Navigating a Fractured Life of Fear

AMY LYNN
As Told to Michele Accardi Shriver

First Printing, 2020
Oceanside Publishing

Contact: Amy.nfear1023@gmail.com
Cover and Formatting: Streetlight Graphics

ISBN 13: 978-1-0957-5498-6
ISBN 10: 1-0957-5498-X

Disclaimer

To protect the identity, and privacy of the real people in this book the characters portrayed have been assigned fictitious names with the exception of the main characters, Charlie, Amy Lynn, and Ceaira. All other aliases have absolutely no connection to any individuals outside the scope of this work. The protagonist has diligently worked to recreate events, locales, and conversations to the best of her recollection throughout a span of almost fifty years. All the events are 'as told to the writer' who had been presented with the opinions, stories, places, and timelines associated with these memories as best called to mind by the main character at the time of publication.

Dedication

Although it took years to "bear and share" our truth, I dedicate this book to my mom, Grace, whose life struggles were the catalyst and motivation to write my life story. Mom's hope was for individuals who are able to relate to the events may hear a 'drumbeat' from their heart to awaken a fragile spirit.

And, for my precious daughter, Ceaira, who taught me how to love and to love without restraint. My "Angel on High," who sends me a fluttering feather, now and again, to let me know I have not lost her. My darling girl lived by the Beatles song, "ALL YOU NEED IS LOVE." Ceaira is and always will be the center of my universe.

Book One

"There is an extremely powerful force that, so far, science has not found a formal explanation to. It is a force that includes and governs all others and is even behind any phenomenon operating in The Universe and has not yet been identified by us. This universal force is LOVE."

~Albert Einstein,
Letter to his daughter, Liesel

Chapter One
The Beliefs

THIS IS A STORY OF love, fear, tragedy, knowledge, acceptance, sorrow, redemption, and of something larger than oneself. It is not a story of religion. It is a personal recollection of my real-life events transcending years of abuse, violation, crime, and other offenses within a family unit, affecting each and every member with callous intent and future consequences to those associated with these misdeeds. At times throughout this story some people will rationalize I had a mental breakdown. Let me assure you, I was and am sane. However, I will leave the scrutiny open to the individuals able to relate to my story. This is not a book of persuasion.

As the years have fled by, I came to realize the events, decisions, and choices of the individual's closest to me, before and after my birth, influenced every aspect of my future life. My entire existence, actually, each day, moment and second have been the result of the actions and events of these predecessors. To blame the people involved would be unfair to them and me. Circumstances, logic, and emotion play a huge role in one's life. I just happen to be a beneficiary.

I wonder if others realize their lives have been affected by the random acts and choices of the ancestral chain. Many may have traveled a similar path, where a descendant's past actions provide their progeny, a future plagued with uncertainty, chaos and misery. What I have finally come to realize is no matter the abuses, tragedies, and losses each of us experience 'love' is the predominant requirement to exist in this unpredictable world. And, 'love' is entirely between the God of one's understanding, oneself *The Universe* and our relationship with human beings. My belief is giving more love equals less strife.

This is my story, and the past has profoundly affected my future. I have not exaggerated the events; although, skeptics may believe otherwise. As I said I am not here to convince anyone. What I share is real, and the timelines are as accurate as witnessed by me. If the incidents did not personally affect me, there would be no story to share. In retrospect, I wish most of what I share had never occurred, except for the birth of my children, Ceaira and Jesse, the sudden vision of a loved one who visited me during a time of great difficulty, and what I perceive as my encounters with The Highest Being. Yes, you read correctly, The Highest Being.

Why I was chosen to endure the insanity of my family or witness the unusual, and other phenomenons is a complete mystery to me. My life has been complicated and, at times, tragic; nevertheless, I realize I am not alone. Everyone has a story. I am sure many have lived in a house where abominable events ran rampant or perhaps witnessed the same experiences as me. Most, if not all of us, have faced abuse, tragedy or loss; however, I do believe there is a select group of us who have witnessed phenomenal visions or observed devine events. This story may comfort and ease the pain and suffering of individuals laying claim to incomprehensible experiences throughout their years. I have a feeling the numbers are in the multitudes. Understandably, to ask people to share their history of observing abuse, violence, and random appearances of spiritual beings is surely intrusive and utterly painful to relive.

Many of us have the ability and strength to overcome life's difficulties and tragedies. Grief, at times, leaves the movement of the human spirit paralyzed, and the soul fractured to do what is right. Many individuals are able to ignore to the point of denial the deviant behavior of individuals close to them. Why? There are spirits who have lost confidence in themselves and continue to accept a life of misery controlled by the abuser. Perhaps the human soul is so weak they cower in fright rather than choose not to be victimized by the wickedness of the perpetrator or others who resemble him or her. I cannot tell you how many times I observed the beatings by Lenny, my stepfather, inflicted upon my mother when in progress. Desperation leaves us hopeless; addictions abound, suicide happens more often than we care to acknowledge. Do we not realize we have the power to live life without the incomprehensible acts of a habitual offender? It took my mother, Grace, years to believe she was a person of worth, and it happened in a most unusual way.

My life's story has been bizarre with many obstacles and twists. During the formative years, I tried to understand the chaotic thoughts I had gathered in the recesses of my naive brain regarding the crazy family with whom I lived. When events around the house escalated into madness in my muddled head I conjured up and directed an incredible imaginary film. As each unconscionable act became too unbearable, this fantasy film became a somewhat therapeutic outlet, where hope for a positive thoughtful solution to end the chaos was desired. Sadly, it was not my all-time favorite movie.

Over and over, the scene remained the same. I visualized myself sitting in a train car while on a roller coaster ride. My brain cells surrounded and protected by an imaginary gauntlet. No one but me had the power to access the unbearable thoughts. Within the fantasy gauntlet, I hoped I could sort out the strange instances of abuse and dysfunction in my family's house. If there was a place in my brain where happy found a place, I often missed the scene. The struggle to find a sense of peace, love, and normality in my dysfunctional young world became an ongoing obsession. If the made-up movie paralleled my life, I most often mentally plunged to the bottom of the fierce roller coaster's decline with no resolution to my ongoing family life dilemma. Would I ever hope to find some sense of stability and survive this physical world where I existed? My entire family's lives were in shambles. Never would there be intervention, or resolution. I was simply navigating the path of my life without support. Occasionally, I found myself wrapped in total fear or worry for my loved ones; or perhaps I or my mother would be mortally wounded by my psychopath stepfather.

Millions of electrical currents fighting for understanding attempted to rationalize the undesirable, strange and abnormal madness surrounding my unpredictable, disturbed, and unfavorable family life. The main question, always, "What is a normal family?" If only my brain cells were able to find reasonable answers and solutions to the random daily acts of lunacy and tragic events surrounding my fractured existence. Perhaps security and comfort would be in reach. You, know, like how real families live in their home. It would have been eventful for Dad and Mom to come home after work enjoying family meals and discussions around the dinner table. What would it be like? It was not like that at all. Mom sat at attention around the table with the kids at mealtime. Lenny, my stepfather never left the bedroom during mealtime. However, mom sadly waited to be summoned by the brute who demanded my mom serve him where he lay. Yes, he surely was good at laying there.

We did not speak in a whispered voice at mealtime for fear the tyrant would rise from his supine position to use a backhander, or worse on the person he thought spoke to loudly. Most of the time it appeared futile to make sense of a complicated home life where the residents seemed mentally unsound. Staying normal in an abnormal home became a daily challenge. In my own way and in my mind, always with the best intentions, I navigated a personal course of survival to make changes in my absurd life. My brain's circuitry needed to take charge to re-calibrate and make sense of all the confusion it held. This was always an immense challenge.

During the younger years the made-up movie seemed to parallel my existence with rare highs and frequent lows. I always had faith to find answers to life's inequities at the end of the trains fierce decline. Many times, I felt fear when the jarring vehicle in my fantasy movie began to plummet to the bottom or end of the trip. At other times, as I plummeted toward the end, I was filled with hope and the notion there would be a credible solution to the daily mania. During the phantasmal journey I held fast there would appear a wise and beneficent *Genie out of the Bottle*. This Entity would have all the answers to the questions in my muddled head regarding my uncertain, and severely flawed family. Perhaps the *Genie, using* its wisdom would help me to understand and give solace to my overwrought thoughts regarding the menacing people in my family's house. Yes, peace of mind would emerge like a *Genie out of the Bottle*. Finally, enveloped in security, in a stable environment; the outrageous madhouse where I lived would become a place of humanness. In truth, my family was aberrant. Nothing would ever change.

When finally, able to emancipate myself from the dysfunctional family house, I was barely an adult and noticeably pregnant. The blessed unplanned event was the solution to advance my escape plan. Shortly after the news was leaked to my mother and stepfather, I moved in with my boyfriend, Harley, and his family. With the departure, I became willful and persistent and worked diligently to affect a normal and perfect life. For a time, I found freedom and was able to somewhat invent the future I yearned. The blessed event produced the happiest newborn baby girl I could have imagined and loved. I relished being a mother and was totally in love with my child. I believed I had reached the pinnacle to complete a perfect life, Yet, my challenges did not end there. At the time I did not realize I was just at the beginning of a lifelong unimaginable rollercoaster ride. The continuation of my journey with highs and plunging lows.

Book Two

Chapter Two
The Beginnings

I AM GETTING AHEAD OF MYSELF. Allow me to start at the beginning way back to my birth, or perhaps before the event. My existence began sweet. I know I was loved while in the womb and for a time after I arrived. During the first ten months of my life, I had wonderful parents, Charlie and Grace, who adored and gave me all the nurturing and security a child needed. We were the perfect little family. My mother, Grace, repeated this *truth* to me many times during her life.

To start at the beginning is the only way the ride, or voyage is to be understood; although my existence began sweet the road was rife with a myriad of unfortunate circumstances and complexities. Now I realize the excursion was all about getting me ready for the ultimate challenge. I just never anticipated there was a plan, a plan already in place made by a *Power* greater than me. Dysfunctional and violent daily occurrences do not help prepare one for a future of severe crisis or tragedy. Or would they?

Nor would rational souls believe I encountered strange visions where I communicated with a long-passed loved one and a *Higher Power*. During the time of my unexplainable experiences, I am guessing most psychiatrists or medical doctors would have perhaps discounted a story of powers *greater than myself*. Assuredly, these icons of medical excellence would have diagnosed this girl with PTSD; or labeled me mentally disturbed and prescribed a plethora of psychotropic drugs to help reconcile what they believed to be an unreal phenomenons. However, neither was true. I know I was and am in my right mind. It is merely my conviction most of us only have a rudimentary understanding of a *Higher Power* or the extraordinary. Until one experiences the unknown, as I have, the reality of the unbelievable shall continue to be a mystery.

In the early years I begged to understand all of my ongoing imaginary life movies. When I was an infant it did not take long for the sweetness of loving parents surrounding me to end. Thereafter, in the ensuing months and years the people closest to me, as well as myself were lodged in an insane house of madness. As an adult when I exited the tumultuous part of my mother's life and left her to struggle by herself, there were years I faced a myriad of problems with relationships. To ask others to believe the encounters I experienced were a series of unthinkable, fearful, or awe-inspiring observations is all about another's ability to recognize; and accept a person's strange, painful and otherworldly events. You can decide the "Truth." I have already acknowledged my belief.

Although eventually, the greatest fear of my life found its way to cripple my thinking. And, it wasn't all! From beginning to end of my story, two forces were helping me to navigate the critical moments of my life. When these extraordinary apparitions appeared, their presence kept me from plummeting into a never-ending well of despair. One, a vision of an unexpected loved one I never knew in the physical world. The other, call it a *Higher Power*, God, The Divine, or Jesus. Call this Entity whatever is wished. However, I knew it was bigger than *The Universe*.

Truth is stranger than fiction
But it is because Fiction is obliged to stick to possibilities
Truth isn't.

~Mark Twain

Book Three

Chapter Three
My Beloved Dad

I WAS BORN AMY LYNN WHALEY on October 23, 1971 to Charlie Casford and Grace Whaley. A child of the balanced scales; or perhaps on the cusp. Born on the cusp of October could have changed up my character a bit. Perhaps this may be the reason I did not go insane. I believe this may, I say 'may' be determined by the stars. One wonders? I am not giving credence here. I am just saying. Whaley was my mother's maiden name as my parents were not married at the time of my birth. My mom told me it was a beautiful sunny fall day when I entered this world in Camden, New Jersey. She said the leaves were brilliantly colored in gold and orange and the air was calm and smelled sweet and full of crisp Fall air. She thought the elements perfect for my birth. When I was brought into the world, my mother was just eighteen, and my father seventeen. Dad was so happy about the birth of his newborn baby he drove through the neighborhood with all the car windows down yelling, "IT'S A GIRL! IT'S A GIRL!" Mom said, he was beyond excited. However, the young in love pair were themselves just teenagers. Sort of a silly thing to do.

My mother Grace said my birth was a blessing for her. She related to me her childhood was tough. She was reared by two alcoholic parents. My birth allowed her to be free from her dreadful life. Since my father was only seventeen, mother moved in with my dad to the Casford family home. A year later my parents were married, and I was given my father's last name, Casford. Although very young, they were desperately in love with each other. How they met is typical for kids who live in the same neighborhood. My dad was a friend of mom's brother, Michael. He always hung around the Whaley's garage and enjoyed taking part in fixing the lines of automobiles waiting to be repaired. Dad was tall, slight of build, and attractive. They became fast friends and after a while, dad invited Mom to take long walks through the neighborhood, usually back and forth from her house to his home. He was so mild-mannered and caring, and mom was totally enamored with his calm, friendly nature. Since both her parents were usually intoxicated, and daily explosions of violence and never-ending chaos were regular, his companionship gave her respite from the turbulent house where she lived.

When they walked by dad's house, two of his brothers, Martin and Brian, who were usually lazing on the porch steps, teased them so badly she wanted to cringe. As young boys, they continuously yelled, "Charlie has a girlfriend," and other childish comments. Mom said dad was so sweet he just brushed off the nonsense.

One Sunday, while both were supposedly on their way to church, dad changed the plan and borrowed the family car. He wanted to buy mom a puppy. Unfortunately, he did not notice the rear license plate was half hanging off its bolts. A patrolman did. They were pulled over. Dad, at seventeen, did not have a driver's license. The patrolman immediately took the two to the police station and the teenagers were justly punished and not allowed to see each other.

My grandfather, dad's father, wheeled out a brilliant disciplinary action. He had dad remove an entire engine from an automobile, clean all the parts and place the enormous equipment back in the vehicle. Mom said, "dad actually enjoyed the punishment and made light of it." She was a little precocious and sneaked out of the house at night, and usually walked to the garage where dad worked. While with my dad, she handed him tools and learned a great deal about mechanics. So much so, I often wondered why when her future life became unbearable, she did not pursue mechanics as a trade. During the dreadful times in her life with Lenny perhaps she was too young, depressed, or naïve of the social stigma defined by society. A lady mechanic? Not too smart! Sometimes, we women sell ourselves short. The times are not always in favor of one's abilities or desires to take on an unconventional skill. This was the Seventy's and certainly not the norm for a girl living in Camden, New Jersey. Opinions were different then. At least for her, I suppose, it seemed so.

Apparently, as young as dad was, he earned a reputation as a hard and diligent worker. His job as a mechanic earned him extra money on the side working on people's cars. Dad saved enough to reach his goal to buy a house for my mom and me. She was the happiest she had ever been in her life.

Unfortunately, the joy of living a family life together for my loving parents ended abruptly. When dad was eighteen, he had a third job working late at night as a street sweeper. It was a lonely job and difficult at times to stay awake. He usually took along a companion to talk to. At times mom wrapped me in a snuggly blanket and took me along with dad for the night street sweep. She loved to accompany him while he ran the big machine, and I quietly slept the night away in her arms. To this day, I am so comforted by these memories she shared with me.

Dad had seven siblings, and if Mom was unable to ride with him, he asked one of his brothers to go along. On this particular evening, he was planning to take my mom, but I was sick and crying a great deal, and mom decided to keep me comfortable and stay home. Two of dad's brothers wanted to go along with him the fateful evening. Martin was older at fifteen, and Brian was thirteen. The two brothers began to argue about who was to be the co-pilot on tonight's ride. Dad had to decide who the lucky one would be. He said, Brian could go along this time since he was the youngest and had not ridden the street sweeper in a long time. Martin did not like my dad's decision and became terribly angry. He stayed behind and yelled at the brothers, "I hate you! I hope you die!" I know my Uncle Martin regretted those words for the rest of his life.

My mom's hellacious life would continue and become pitiful and denigrated from the ranks of hell on this day. On the way to work, while driving his car my dad and Uncle Brian were hit head-on by a drunk driver with four inebriated men in the out of control vehicle. The driver was never charged. My Uncle Brian died instantly. Dad's mangled body and his lifeless brother were transported to the hospital. With critical injuries, but a strong body the physicians believed he would survive. When I was old enough to understand, I was told after my mother received the fateful call telling her of the accident she immediately rushed to his bedside. My dad's mom, Grandmother Leona, through her brokenness and with her sons' and mom's fate lingering, stayed with the young girl and both sat with dad, and prayed for hours. When Mom finally stepped out of the room for a minute, to regroup and recall her breath to a slight awareness, dad awakened. He was confused and severely injured, however, and asked his mom, "Where are Grace and Amy. Are they OK?" Terribly disoriented he thought we had been in the street sweeper with him. When Mom walked back into the room, he remembered and asked about his brother, Brian. They were unable to tell him Brian had died, and just said, "Brian will be OK." Dad fell back into a deep sleep. The doctor told my mom and grandmother to go home and get some rest. Both had planned to return to the hospital early the next morning. Regretfully, it was the last time they would see my dad alive.

During the night, a blood clot from his injuries traveled to his heart and killed him while he was sleeping. My mom received a call from the hospital and listened to the words she never wanted to hear. Poor Grandmother Leona lost two sons that fateful night. My mom lost the love of her life, and I missed a life with the wonderful dad I never knew or got to know. My dad, Charlie Casford died on March 5th, 1973.

After my dad died, my mother hit a downward spiral. And, the events following were the ruination for most of her future life. Our paths were about to drastically change, and we were to begin to live in a frightful and violent home dominated by an evil human being. I will refer to these living conditions as *The House of Madness*.

A thousand times we needed you
A thousand times we cried
If love alone could have saved, you
you never would have died
A heart of gold stopped beating
two twinkling eyes closed to rest
God broke our hearts to prove
he only took the best
never a day goes by that you're not
in my heart and soul

~Kimberly N. Chasten, Author

Chapter Four
Lenny – "The House of Madness"

U NFORTUNATELY, ALL THE TRAGEDIES, HEARTACHES, and struggles began with my mother. After my father died, she could not afford the lovely home my father had bought for their little family. For a second time Grandmother Leona offered her home, and for a while she stayed with the Casford's. Regrettably we did not live there very long. Within several months after my dad passed, mom began to see a man, a friend of the Casford's extended family. He appeared to show up without invitation or warning. The miscreants name was Lenny Martel. Mom was now twenty years old, and Lenny was twenty-one. At the time, several members of the Casford family married Martel's. Giving the impression he was comforting my mom while she mourned my dad; he also appeared to genuinely care for her and vowed to do anything to ease her grief. Lenny was very handsome and charming. Tall and well-built with dark hair, Mom, who was an incredibly lonely and a bereaved woman, was ideal prey for a hunter such as this man.

Although young and beautiful, she was also vulnerable, naive, broke, and terribly broken. She fell for the security offered by this charismatic evildoer. Lenny's comforting also included sex. Mom again became pregnant. She now felt strange living with the Casford family while being in this state, with another man's child. At this time, I was only three years old. She did not know how to care for another man's baby and me while living at the Casford's. This fragile woman was frightened and soon realized how desperate her life had become.

It was not long before Lenny asked my mom to marry him. Grandmother Leona had reservations about the forthcoming nuptial's to Lenny. She did not believe he was a truthful or loyal person and did not trust him. Grandmother tried to encourage my mom to stay with her, and she would help with the new baby. Mom was confused, young, and unable to make the right decisions. At the time, Lenny's charisma overtook her logic. She did not know how evil this man could be. Apprehensive to be left unwed with a new baby, she decided to marry this horrible, maladjusted brute. The event catapulted my dear, naïve mother into a life where not only she, but other family members, witnessed and suffered abuse, alcoholism, chaos, betrayal, and the misconduct of a sexual predator.

When their life together began, Lenny had a good job in a factory as a welder. I suppose at the beginning of mom's and Lenny's relationship economics was the tradeoff my mother accepted for all the past suffering. We left Grandma Leona's and moved in with Lenny. I was about five years old when sadly lodged in *The House of Madness*. According to my mom the physical and verbal abuse began immediately. My brother, Larry was finally born in 1975. Within a few months, mom was on her way with another pregnancy. My sister Jenna was born in 1976. My brother, Ray followed in 1978. After a few years together, Lenny was able to buy a small house for his family in Pennsauken, New Jersey.

We were living in the new little house for a year when mom decided to help her sister, my Aunt Angie, who was fourteen. Like my mom, Aunt Angie had also been raised in a desperate situation while living at my maternal grandmother's home. Unfortunately, her parents' house, along with the alcoholism was also a place of abuse where, not surprisingly, chaos was an everyday event. In the past my dad, Charlie, had saved my mom. Aunt Angie was mom's only sister, and she feared for her safety. Her hope had been to prevent Aunt Angie from a future life of disaster.

The day before Aunt Angie moved in, mom stopped by her mother's house and found Aunt Angie and her youngest brother, Vince, snuggled together on the floor with blankets piled on them while trying to keep warm. There was no heat or electricity. Mom's siblings were freezing. She had a terrible time sleeping through the night, knowing her siblings were living in these conditions. Also, no food was found for the children to eat, but, surely, an abundant amount of booze was in sight for adult consumption. Although mom was subject to Lenny's tirades and routinely dealt with abuse, she believed she was so lucky to have the luxury of food and shelter.

The next day she gathered up Aunt Angie, and the young teen became part of our chaotic family. She wished she could have also helped Vince, but Lenny was not going to let it happen. Mom had older brothers and hoped they would somehow come to Vince's rescue. As little as I was when I first saw Aunt Angie, I remember she looked disheveled, and her clothing was too big for her. I thought she looked odd and to me seemed a sad, scared, teen girl. Since the house in Pennsauken was so small, we had to make room for our new family member. In time, my brother Larry and I were eventually relocated to the attic. Despite the fact it was an unfinished space mom did the best she could to make it a bedroom, it was still an attic.

Book Four

Chapter Five
The Vision

"Then he turned to his disciple and said privately,
"Blessed are the eyeshot see what you see".

~Luke 10:23

W HEN ABOUT EIGHT YEARS OLD, a few months after moving to the attic, the phenomena, vision or dream became a reality somewhere in the middle of sleep. Personally, I need to call it an apparition turned into my reality. Although, I never knew or remembered my real father's face, apparently, he knew me. I had no idea what he looked like. Lenny had destroyed most of the photos of my dad, and my mom was not allowed to talk about or keep pictures of him. I guess she did not realize Lenny's obsessive and jealous nature early on in their relationship.

Since the attic took up the entire top of the house, it had ample space. There was a squeaky stairway, and upon entering the room to the right loomed a large window. The window is an essential feature in understanding my experience. Here, I was in the attic in my bed, somewhere between the sleep cycle and, suddenly, in the frame of the vast enclosure, was an image of my father. I knew it was him because words came from his mouth and during the appearance, he told me so. Yes, I believe this vision is an actual manifestation of my dad's human embodiment. His words to me during the night are permanently implanted in the cells of my brain. He told me how much he loved me, how he would be watching over me forever and to always think of him when life was terrible, and he would forever protect me. Then the image faded away with him saying 'it was time for him to move on. And, although I would never see him again, he would never leave me'.

I believed, and am convinced to this day, the vision of my father was real. Perhaps a phenomenon to others; his appearance was absolutely real to me. My dad, who is somewhere in *The Universe*, must have known how tough my life would be. I believe he knew Lenny to be an evil force in my life for many years. I have been privy to many horrendous experiences in *The House of Madness*. Although, I regularly experienced fear and verbal abuse as well as strange disciplinary measures; I did not personally experience the physical, violent, and sexual abuse my mother and others in my household endured. I also believe my dad's appearance during the rough times resulted in my ability to initiate personal survival skills, not always perfect; however, giving me the mental ability to 'march on' to brave future crisis, and keep me somewhat grounded.

When I awakened the next morning, tears streamed down my face. For me the vision I had, screamed reality. Shrouded in love from dad's visit, and his appearance left me feeling protected and joyful. I did not want the wonderful joy to end. And I will never forget the face and persona of my loving dad. His eyes were brown, as was the color of his shaggy hair. He was clothed in a navy-blue shirt with white buttons running down the front opening. The morning after the event, I excitingly ventured downstairs to the kitchen and told my mother what I had experienced. She was shocked and, asked if I was sure he wore a navy-blue shirt? I said, "Yes, Mom, navy blue with white buttons down the front." She started to cry and said it was exactly what your dad was wearing the night he died. I know my dad was speaking to me during one of the most incredible evenings of my life. It was fantastical and real. This is the only good memory I have while living in *The House of Madness*.

My son, Jesse, looks a lot like my father. At age thirteen tall and thin, he topped at six feet. My dad was six foot and three inches. Jesse has shaggy hair like his Grandpa, but more blond. Charlie and he have the same eyes. When I see found pictures of my dad, they resemble each other so much, it is scary. I cannot help but wonder if God lets our loved one's soul come back again to be with us in another's body. I guess we will never know. Frequently during the years, my son Jesse has nightmares about being in a car crash. He wakes up frightened and tells me about it. I wonder!

Chapter Six
Mom's Strange Life with Lenny

LENNY WAS ALWAYS A SCARY man. Never did he display any affection for me or any of my siblings, including the children from his own loin. He was devious and cruel, and never talked to me unless I did something wrong. Until I moved out of his house, I was terrified of this evil person. In all the eighteen years I lived with him, never once, did he hug, comfort, or give me advice or any positive words of wisdom. Since my mom had such a bad childhood, I do not believe she ever received any affection, except with my dad in the short time they were together. And, I believe after my dad died part of her soul died with him. As a child, I don't remember her ever hugging or telling me she loved me, although I feel she may have. However, it was probably so random I cannot really remember. Obviously, it was not a feeling enough for me to recognize. And, coupled with the loss of my dad, after so many beatings from the evildoer, Lenny, she was unable to show affection toward me or her other children. Also, since Lenny was so jealous of my father, and I was the product of the love they shared, I realize she was too afraid to show me love.

Mom was never allowed by Lenny to attend any of my school events, including my graduation from high school. All the other parents were always present congratulating and supporting their children's milestones, but I was alone. Coming from a dysfunctional house, you just sort of let the important events slip by and only think abstractedly about where you are and what you are doing. And, give others the most unbelievable excuses as to why your parents are not in attendance. It was heartbreaking and disappointing to me; so, I gave myself an excuse I could handle. There was no reason to try to make sense of his actions. He merely ruled as he wished, with fear. This isolation was all I knew. It was perpetually living in a House of Madness, with dread, never love.

My mom paid for any violation of Lenny's rules whether committed by her or any of the other children. As a witness to so many horrible experiences, growing up to share the story of living a fractured life has always been a personal torture. Stability was not a strong suit for me. Sometimes I was in control of my emotions, at other times I failed. Failing came in waves of bad choices, especially in future relationships. However, no matter how adverse circumstances became, I always knew from the time of the vision of my dad in the attic window, I could make it through. I believe God, as well as, my dad was indeed with me through the worst times.

When Aunt Angie moved into our home, I noticed throughout the time, my stepfather, Lenny, gave her a great deal of attention, usually when my mother was absent. I am sure she loved the favoritism since she came from an abusive, dysfunctional home. Angie was a relatively quiet girl. Her time was mostly spent reading Stephen King novels and romance books. She watched television and slept a lot. Angie was not mean. At least not in the beginning. I believe I saw her as being melancholy and incredibly naïve.

I was about eight years old when I first witnessed a scene; it was and still is a permanent, mental photograph imprinted deep inside my cerebral hemisphere. And, unfortunately, it is still retrievable at any triggered moment. Walking in on my stepfather, Lenny, and a not quite fifteen-year-old Aunt Angie, I witnessed them kissing and embracing. And, while I secretly looked on, he molested and explored her body. It thoroughly confused my fragile child's soul. Although the two did not see me the first time there were many instances where I was exposed to the disturbing scenes of sexual misconduct where an adult took advantage of a minor. Each time I witnessed the disturbing scenes I usually ran out of the house so fast acting as natural as possible. And, each of them was guilty of betrayal, but Lenny was the adult, and I was frightened to death of being caught as the observer. One wonders if the stress of the scene I had captured left me way too willing to take some irresponsible chances without worry of outcome.

As time went on, I continued to witness abnormal sexual behavior between my Aunt Angie and Lenny. When Lenny was home, he stayed in his room most of the time. The master bedroom was adjacent to the living room. Aunt Angie usually sat on the couch watching TV. I remember many occasions when my mom was not at home, Lenny knocked on his bedroom wall three times. This was Aunt Angie's cue to join him on my mother's side of her bed. By then I was fully aware of what was happening in my mother's bedroom and in her bed; and, I was too distraught to say anything. I hated this time at home witnessing Lenny's betrayal of my mother. Aunt Angie could not have realized she was sexually abused. I believe she thought she was in love, and felt she was being loved.

"Anyone who has no need of anybody
but himself is either a beast or a God."

~Aristotle

Book Five

Chapter Seven
My Best Friend Carene

AT LEAST I HAD MY friend Carene. We met in pre-school and spent a lot of time swinging on swings together at the playground. In grade school, we made it a point to sit next to each other in all our classes. When we were old enough to walk to each other's houses to play, I called her on the telephone, and we met halfway. Just the sight of Carene made me feel so happy and sane. She always greeted me with the biggest smile. Carene was a beautiful young girl, tall and graceful with long black shiny hair. I remember comparing a mole on her left cheek with Marilyn Monroe's. And, telling her on several occasions I thought someday she would probably be a model. I loved fixing her hair and makeup and promised when she became famous, I would be her travel and cosmetic assistant, and we would become wealthy adults. I guess my vocation took effect early. I became an aesthetician. But I never grew rich, and she never became a famous model.

Carene's family treated me very well. Her mom frequently invited me to dinner. I spent many overnights at her home, and many times her family paid for tickets for me to accompany the family to Great Adventure. Before one of our trips, I sent Carene a letter. I had been obsessing about how to pay for the journey and what concessions I needed to make. I made a copy of this letter. Carene thought she would send the letter back to me since, at the time, it was so crucial in my life. In it, I asked her if I should sell my Michael Jackson memorabilia, or buy more Duran Duran. The funny things we say as children.

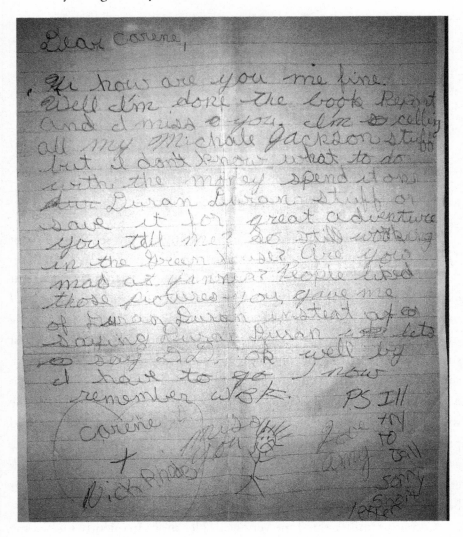

Letter to Carene

Carene's family realized my mom did not allow, nor did she have any money to permit entertainment. At times her mom took me along to the mall to buy clothes and shoes for me. The family was not wealthy; however, they were aware we were a poor family, or thought we were poor.

In reality Carene's mom knew I was treated poorly. There was an older brother, Jeff. He was delightful and loved to pick on us in a fun way. I remember having snowball fights with Jeff and his sister. It was unusual for me to interact with any young male outside my house. These two siblings were the only friends who were sincere and non-judgmental of my strange home life. With Carene and Jeff, I imagined myself as part of a healthy family with normal siblings.

Now, when I think of my ordinary, wished-for family, it seems so tragic to have found it necessary to replace my 'real' tragic family. Carene's mom was always worried about me. She knew there were issues in my home but was not sure what they were. I kept most of the dysfunction from the people I was close to for fear I would be ostracized. If she knew what was really going on at my house, I may have forever lost Carene's friendship. I am not sure she could have placed her daughter in such a dysfunctional environment if she had had been aware of the vicious beatings my mother was accustomed to, or Lenny's sexual proclivity with Aunt Angie.

Another concern for Carene's mother was the new job I had packing corn at a nearby farm. For a fourteen-year-old, it was a long ride on my bicycle at five o'clock in the morning when the roads were still dark. But I was used to working and had had another job picking blueberries when I was thirteen. Never was I afraid to extend my energy to make more money. Luckily, Carene's mother acted as my second mom consistently worrying about my safety. I was so grateful for the comfort and normalcy at my friend's family home. It was my refuge and escape from the abuse, chaos, violence, as well as the sexual acts performed by Lenny on my minor aunt.

Lenny did not complain too much about my relationship with Carene. I guess he was aware we were together all the time, day and night, and she helped so much with the other children in *The House of Madness*. It appeared the miscreant simply decided to ignore us just as he had my siblings. Lenny was not a father, just a tyrant! We were all non-entities, and his biological children, unfortunately, were only the results of his seed.

Angel Without Wings

"Our friends are Angels
so precious and priceless
and cherished, too
for all that they give
and all that they do;
For their hearts provide us with love,
and their smiles provide us with hope
their warmth gives us comfort
And, I want you to know
You're all these beautiful things to me
and I'm so glad you're my friend
an Angel without wings."

– The Poetry Pad

Book Six

Chapter Eight
Finding My "Real" Family Home

WHEN I WAS ELEVEN YEARS old, my dad's family had asked my mom to allow me to visit their home. She was so afraid of Lenny; it took her a long time to agree after many requests from the Casford's. I also later learned one of my dad's brothers had had a conversation with Lenny. I assume he got right to the point. Apparently, he knew Lenny was a sexual predator. Finally, Lenny relented. Why? I have no idea! My guess is he didn't want anyone outside the *brick and wood* to be aware of what everyone in the house knew. And, perhaps he thought giving me this privilege would assure him a sense of loyalty.

When occasionally able to visit my grandparents' home, I loved being with all my dad's relatives, who embraced me with their kindness and affection. Finally, I met my cousin Susan who was about my age, and we were like sisters. And my Aunt Louise, my dad's sister, and Susan's mom, acted as another mom for me. I considered myself so lucky and grateful to finally have a relationship with my real dad's family. Grandmother Leona showed me so much love; I wallowed in happiness. Granddad Finne was so full of jokes. I laughed all the time. Many times, he took me to McDonald's. At twelve years old, I had never been there before. During these precious times, granddad was the only adult male figure in my life who was a positive influence, and he made me feel safe. Finally, I was able to see pictures of my loving father and hear beautiful stories about him.

Sadness always crept up on me when I returned to the *madhouse*. If there was only a way I could disappear from the crazy bunch and never be around them. Again, when taken away from dad's family, I was left terribly unhappy, forever enveloped in mental pain and fear. Eventually, strength and determination took over enough to beg and cry until I got my way to be with my 'real family' more often. I stayed strong and resilient. My hard work to rid me of fear paid off. Lenny finally capitulated, and my mom who also had problems parting with me for long periods of time had no say. Although, Lenny knew I was old enough to wash the filthy family laundry away from his house, he may have finally realized by allowing me to visit the Casford's more regularly, I would not speak of the cruelties, and deviant sex and other mistreatments where I lived. Fractionally emancipated, he had let the raccoon out of the cage. She was alive and well, and she was not going to be trapped any longer. I had the ultimate escape, my dad's family. However, I was still a child and under Lenny's rule. Cautiousness was always my mental sidekick.

Chapter Nine
Back At "The House of Madness"

ALTHOUGH I WAS GETTING A little older and still living at home, the relationship between my stepfather and Angie was becoming more and more deplorable. He began to call her Queen, and she called him King. At one point, Angie had a queen playing card tattooed on her shoulder. My mother should have been the Queen of her home. In a way, she was Queen, the Queen of Fools. I was sickened by the sexual acts going on casually in my mother's or more truthfully Lenny's house between Angie and the reprobate. He surely had to be one of God's rejects. During those times I wondered if my mother was aware, or was she just playing the fool to keep us all safe. Still only a young teen, it was a young person's intuition telling me my mother was scared to death of Lenny. I can't imagine sleeping with the devil, but she had.

One morning while up in my attic room, I decided to come down to watch television. My mom must have been at the grocery store. Lenny and Angie were again having sex on the couch in the living room. This time I could not take it anymore. Confused and horrified I made decision. I knew It would result in a disciplinary action by Lenny; however, I determined a young person should not be witness to blatant acts of sex performed by her stepfather, especially on her underage aunt.

As young as I was, and as afraid of the punishment I shared the events of betrayal of her husband to one's own mom. My heart was tortured, but it was time to tell. When alone with her, I shared all I had heard and seen.

Apparently, at the moment mom mustered up the courage and relayed this information to Lenny. Mistake!

On the same day I related Lenny's sins to my mom he pulled me by the ear and dragged me outdoors. Pulling the ears was one of the abuse measures and punishments inflicted and endured by all of us when the brute was angry. He told me, "you better never tell your mother anything like that again or something bad is going to happen to you." I was sent to my room and told to plant my face. Planting one's face was another punishment he devised. It meant pushing the front of the face into a pillow and not looking up until the sentence he delivered was over. This unbearable treatment could last for hours.

After the incident, the cruel vengeful punishment inflicted by Lenny became a routine for me anytime the evildoer wanted to have sex with Angie. Many days I lay in my bed, face-planted, while unthinkable acts of sex between Lenny and Angie were performed secretly on the living room couch or in the master bedroom. During those years of his betrayal to my mom, I vowed never to repeat anything. As usual, I quietly and silently prayed to God for an end to the devious acts of deception. Lenny and Angie's relationship commenced with freedom and frequency.

Then, suddenly after years of abuse, and mistreatment my mother was no longer in denial. She previously ignored the entire issue. And finally, simply accepted the abnormal situation. I am not even sure if at the time she realized Lenny was a sexual predator or also perhaps a nymphomaniac. He was lethal. She knew it and continued to fear the monster, but apparently thought she had no way out. Mom was burdened with children, no money, and low self-esteem. The beast believed it was his duty to physically abuse her for any small rule ordained by him she may have broken. He considered any incident in the family home the fault of my mom. It didn't matter the cause, or the person involved. If the event appeared unsatisfactory to him, my mother endured his wrath. Sadness and worry were my constant companions in my growing years. At times, physically witnessing the abuse in *The House of Madness* left me emotionally paralyzed.

Later in life, I learned Lenny had affairs with other women while still having sex with my mother and Angie. Eventually, one of his secret lovers became pregnant. In my adult years, I learned he had taken desperate measures to rid himself of any responsibility to the woman. Of course, the devil had no conscience. I did not need to be convinced. Although still young I realized sex was an addiction for him and he was evidently unashamed of his obsession. My mother had had all these babies, and Lenny decided to have sex with any woman he chose without protection. It is a miracle she was never infected with STDs.

By the time mom was twenty-six years old, she had had six children. I don't know why she allowed all these pregnancies or did not use birth control. I never asked; nor would have I. It was odd no one in his family or friends ever talked about Lenny's depraved nature. Perhaps most people were afraid of him; or, rather many found it easier to not involve themselves regarding the problems of others.

Lenny had a punching bag in the basement. He liked to box. At times, he held me captive to keep the bag still while he landed punches. During those terrifying times I remembered thinking how easy it would be for him to hurt me. He also had a penchant for drugs. Strange men came and went from our house. They bought drugs from him and took pills and imbibed in liquor while in the basement. When Lenny did drugs, it made him paranoid, and the violence in him became worse. One time, a drug buddy came to the house and Lenny took him down to the hell hole. When they finished indulging themselves with drugs and alcohol, Lenny brought the guy upstairs.

My mom was in the kitchen. Lenny said to the inebriated, drugged man, referring to my mother "Why are you looking over at her?" He continued to badger and bully the guy as he repeated the same words over and over. The spaced-out and dumbfounded man was not looking at my mom. Lenny then said to my mom, "You like him, Grace. You want to be with him?" My mom said, "No Lenny. Calm down." The devil's eyes looked crazed. He then began beating on the guy like the punching bag he forced me to hold for him. The intoxicated man went running through the living room as though he had been pushed along like a giant wave. And throughout the indignity, Lenny continued to beat him until the guy stumbled and faltered and found his way out the front door and down the steps.

When Lenny returned to the kitchen after terrorizing the man, he chased my mom around the table and landed punches on her, then took her head and smashed it against the kitchen window. She was crying and bleeding at the same time. My mom was only about 5'2" and weighed 98 pounds. The devil, on the other hand, was 6 feet tall and 180 pounds. Apparently, mom was no match for this degenerate. Frightened by Lenny's violence, I ran upstairs to my bedroom, hid and continued a litany of prayer.

This cruel maniac was committed to continuously, without warning, physically abusing my mother. The abominable treatment was merely part of her life with Lenny. I was present for many of the beatings. When not viewing the violence, I knew she had been beaten when seeing the black and blue marks tinged with red on her body. He hit her so often throughout her life with him, eventually, she suffered both mentally and physically. The past years of continuous violent, verbal and physical abuse left my mother a shadow of herself for the longest time. Ironically, although I suffered through many ears pulls and face plantings, Lenny never hit me. I always associated the immunity from his physical violence with the vision of my dad. After all, he told me he would still be there to protect me. I believe dad, who is somewhere in *The Universe,* knew I was in for a rough journey.

Other times, Lenny let his fury out on my brothers, but never my sister Jenna. This is a mystery to me. But I am truly grateful she was not another one of his victims. I'm not sure he ever hit Angie. It was always my mom who knew the rage associated with his violence. Apparently, he never had a guilty conscience while he beat and berated anyone in his path. It appeared he thought himself to be the dominant, tyrannical King who could rule with a wielding fist.

During my entire life with my mom and Lenny, she was never allowed to have a friend. And, never permitted me to speak to my dad's family about any of the horrors taking place at her house, and pretty much had no life for herself except having sex whenever Lenny decided; usually ending up pregnant and taking care of the house and meals. What a life! Although it made little difference, she learned early on to keep her mouth shut. However, ironically, once she did have a job, and was allowed to leave the house. It freed her to be away from the scoundrels' power. This seemed to meet Lenny's criteria of control since he kept all the money she earned.

Chapter Ten
Lenny, The Psychopath

THERE WERE TIMES LENNY ACTED as if my dad was still alive. I remember a few instances where he asked me if I had seen my dad during the day. Of course, I said no. Seeing my dad would give the monster just another excuse to beat my mother who was merely a slave for the beast. He was so jealous, and mercurial. I refrained from ever speaking about my dad in his presence. There was something seriously wrong with Lenny, but I was so young. What did I know?

The future revealed some interesting, and disturbing facts regarding the tyrant's personality. While Lenny was in the drug business, it appeared he was not liked by many of his cronies. Crazy incidents happened during those horrible years, causing a great deal of turmoil for him and our family. Apparently, he had sold some harmful drugs to his brother, Michael. Although it was never admitted by his family, the drugs killed the young man. Michael was found on the floor of his apartment bathroom. It was estimated he had been dead for three days. As a child, I was told he had an accident and hit his head really hard on the bathroom tub while taking a shower. The trauma of the head injury apparently caused his death. There was never any mention of drugs. Lenny denied selling or giving his brother any substances and blamed another dealer for the sale of drugs to the dead Michael. Up until then, Lenny mostly sold drugs. I believe the accusation by the authorities he was involved, as well as the guilt was more than he could handle, and he began selling less and using more. The authorities had Lenny as one of the players on their list of drug dealers. Somehow, they suspected he was guilty of Michael's death.

There had been an ongoing investigation by Pennsauken, New Jersey, Vice Squad, and Lenny was considered shady. The consensus by the Squad had been Lenny may have also been involved in the death of another person. He was dangerous. And the more insecure Lenny became regarding the investigations, the more my mother sustained beatings. At times he became delusional. There was no end to the madness. Most often he acted and talked crazily about being investigated, usually shouting cruel, and dictatorial phrases to take back power or control. He believed he was untouchable. It seemed I was praying all the time for my mom's safety and constantly worried he would beat her to death. We were prisoners of the abuser, his violence, and madness.

During this time, I also learned, not only had he been fired from his job as a welder due to a possible Workmen's Compensation scam, but also had taken a gun to work and threatened to shoot one of the male employees. He actually knocked the guy out with the gun and warned the guy to stay away from his drug territory making known he intended to be King of the drug dealers. Yes, he again had the audacity to compete in the 'trade'.

One morning, we woke up to a fire in our garage. Lenny loved new and expensive cars. He had recently bought a 1978 Lincoln Continental. I believe whoever decided to take vengeance on him set his car on fire. At another time, my mom had all the kids in the family van and drove us kids to visit her mother. Grandma Muriel who lived in a terrible neighborhood in Camden, New Jersey. Lenny had worked in Camden, a known area to be a rampant enclave with drug activity. Many of the dealers lived there. When we left Grandma Muriel's house, we were in the vehicle not five minutes away, when a fire started under the hood. My mom immediately shuffled all of us out of the van It had been a few minutes after mom was able to clear us safely, and, then completely terrified and anxious, we witnessed a massive explosion. The van was blown to pieces. Luckily or unluckily, we all made it out in time to return *The House of Madness*.

I later learned the reason for the blown-up vehicle was due to Lenny cheating one of the dealers out of drug money. However, the family later also heard there was more to the explosion. Apparently, Lenny set fire to one of the drug dealer's homes to burn the suppliers stash of drugs, and the revenge continued on for both sides. Our family was in the middle of a drug war prompted by Lenny's constant evil doings to people who were more prominent in the trade than him. My life was full of fear every day, and we never knew when the next catastrophe would occur. I continued to pray to God who I assumed was somewhere out there.

Suddenly, not long after his brother's death, Lenny was talking about moving to Medford, New Jersey. The biggest excuse for the next relocation he considered the house in Pennsauken too small for the family. The real reason was Lenny figured he was recommended for a hit and had been determined to find a place where no one knew him. This move allowed him to continue his resourcefulness in the drug trade. Another reason, the relationship between him and Aunt Angie became more apparent, and the community was talking. The young girl now sixteen years old became a willing prisoner in the house with no friends, or ability to socialize. Finally, to his chagrin, he became the laughingstock of the neighborhood. My dad's family also asked if Aunt Angie had a boyfriend. I said, I didn't know. The relationship they had in my mother's house was so depraved and disrespectful to her, my heart broke. I wanted to tell everyone I knew the real truth, but I was paralyzed with terror Lenny would beat or maltreat me.

Book Seven

Chapter Eleven
Escape to Medford

BEFORE ARRIVING IN MEDFORD, AUNT Angie became pregnant by Lenny. As a child, I questioned, myself, "was Aunt Angie's child my cousin or my half stepsibling"? Actually, what would have I called this familial relationship? And, what about my mother's relationship to the child? Should the new baby have been her niece, nephew, or her stepchild? What a convoluted hypocrisy on the part of Lenny. The relocation was actually two-fold. He ran from the law and Aunt Angie's new situation. As the young girl began to show, the people in the neighborhood were aware something strange was going on in the Martel house, and eyes began to roll, and heads began to spin. She hardly left the confines, and no one had ever seen teens or young men hang around this young girl. It was thought by the community, who had a glimpse of the increasing bump, she had a boyfriend in Pennsauken who would not stand by her in her condition. Of course, no one believed the deception. It was many years before the truth was finally told; although the baby, who would be named Hanna, surely had her suspicions as she became older. I detested the lie.

I was almost twelve years old when we moved to Medford, New Jersey. Before Lenny uprooted our family, I had been visiting my real dad's family more frequently where I found peace, solace and love. These visits kept me happy and grounded in deference to the maladjusted household commanded by Lenny. Especially sad, and without my real dad's family close by, and my friend Carene, I was in a sea of loneliness. Moving away from the sanctuary at the Casford's, and my best friend and her family, devastated me. Medford was known to be a community established by and for wealthy residents compared to the working class and the more impoverished neighborhood of Pennsauken. Our chaotic and financially flawed horde of people definitely did not fit in with the community.

Since the investigation into Lenny's crimes were ongoing, he believed the move a safer distance away from the Pennsauken Vice Squad. After the loss of his job and the move to Medford, Lenny became depressed and severely anxious all the time. He learned the police were not as sense-less as he had assumed and stayed hot on his tail. After locating him the detectives continued to question Lenny as a suspect on the same crime issues he had faced in Pennsauken. All these problems simply magnified his chaotic and manic moods. You can run, but you cannot hide. Eventu-ally, you will be found!

At this point, filled with anxiety, and depressed he decided to see a physician. The strange and manic moods were not medical. Lenny had been swiftly diagnosed with paranoid schizophrenia. Really? What a joke! The attending physician prescribed an abundant supply of psychotropic drugs for his treatment. This kept him somewhat quiet. It had also been suggested Lenny use light therapy to help his depression. I later learned the reason for the light treatment was due to a condition called SAD, or Seasonal Affective Disorder. As if his mental illness wasn't enough of a problem for everyone in the family to tolerate, we now had to deal with his environmental issue.

All the way around, the family was now more than ever cloaked in overwhelming dysfunction, chaos, and stress the devil expected sympathy, and servitude in the extremes. I hated him. But my Grandma Leona was so compassionate; she tried to convince me he was just a sick man and could not be held accountable for all of his actions. She also said, "Amy, God does not want you to hate." I didn't buy it, but nevertheless, and at least for a while, I let my mental rankings of anger and resentment submerge itself back into the recesses of my brain. If she only knew!

Ironically, due to his mental disability, Lenny was able to collect Social Security Disability Insurance, and delighted to learn he would receive a check for each of us six kids. As young as I was, I believed him to be a scam artist. In some way, he always managed to cheat the system, schizophrenia or not. At this point the paranoid person now spent ninety percent of his time in his bedroom, the den of evil; or the remaining ten percent quietly, observing the family while prowling the house like the psycho he was. Lenny became a silent, scary, phantom. The calmness acquired by the drugs did not last very long. Life became more distressing for the entire family when he decided not to take his medication. He had severe mood swings and horrible escalating moments of violence bordering on brutal. We lived a constant horror movie of terrifying proportions. Without notice, when not in his room he likened to a jack-in-a box' wielding his hand to every passing family member in our house usually without much cause.

When not reveling outside the house with his friends, or with random girlfriends; although quiet with his voice, he caused significant grief while he played Pink Floyd or Led Zeppelin records so loud our ear drums were almost blown. And, when he wanted to be waited on, he would knock on the wall for my mother, the servant to wait on him. On one occasion, my brother, Larry, was pummeled in the face by Lenny with a red plastic track from a train set. Ok! So, it was plastic. However, he had the track mark on his face for quite a while. At another time my sister Jenna's misdeed caused Lenny to pick her up by one arm, scolding, and shaking her while holding her in the air. There was no getting away from the eruptions associated with Lenny's madness! The brutality was simply a normal part of our abnormal family's lives. And, my mother Grace received ninety-five percent of the rage, beatings.

It wasn't too long after arriving in Medford when Aunt Angie delivered her baby, by Lenny, Hanna. In the new house, there were four bedrooms. My stepbrothers, Ray and Jason shared a room, and stepbrothers, Larry and the new infant, Danny, occupied another. Aunt Angie and Lenny's child, Hanna, and my stepsister Jenna were in the same room. Now there were two infants. My mom's newborn, Danny, and Aunt Angie's newborn, Hanna, both from Lenny. The sleeping quarters were tight. The place was a menagerie. To say there was a level of comfort for all and easy on my mom would be a fallacy.

There was no attic space or basement in this house, however, there was a huge unattached garage in the rear yard. One of Lenny's friends was commissioned to construct a wall and split the area into two with a temporary partition. I became the lodger in one-half of the garage and slept there with the constant and nauseating smell of gasoline from the cars parked in the bay on the other side of a thin wall. It was anything but cozy, warm or comfy. What a joy!

Mom tried to arrange the dark, frigid, neglected area as a more pleasant room for me by placing a carpet on the concrete floor, but she could not help to keep my body from suffering the bitter cold; or stave off the offensive odor. Without access to a bathroom, I had to leave the garage, go outdoors, walk across the lawn and enter the house from outside. If the entrance door was locked, oh well! It was a ludicrous situation.

I descended from a room in the attic of our old home in Pennsauken to a place in the smelly garage with no heat. "This girl learned how to bundle up very well so she would not freeze. Lucky me!" However, living in the garage had one positive effect, it made me feel more secure. Except for my sister, Jenna, I did not want to be in the confines with this dysfunctional bunch. It was so hard to understand these feeling for my siblings whom I loved but could never love our living condition or their father. For some reason, I always felt different from them. And actually, I believed I was. Lenny's blood did not run through my veins. I never belonged there with the family, but I tried my best to adapt to my new surroundings and the significant mayhem in the house. If time and the occasion had permitted, I would have removed all these kids from Lenny's domain. Perhaps all the children may have been spared from the tyrant's abuse, and each may have aspired to a more normal, and successful future. However, I was still a child to young too actually consider freeing myself, or my siblings. We were all trapped. Making waves was out of the question. I chose to harbor all the resentment in my already muddled brain.

Ironically, my mom and Lenny were still sleeping together in the master bedroom. She could not get away from him and his sexual appetite. He commanded two women as sex slaves. One, my mother who was a docile, complicit and frightened woman; and, the other, Aunt Angie, too young, naive and looking for love in *all the wrong places*. At times, if my mom had not been pregnant with a baby of Lenny's, Aunt Angie was. What a joke!

My fragile child's heart was a puzzle of fragmented pieces. And my brain was a self-constructed maze of disturbing thoughts rambling on with no conclusion as to how to help or fix my mom's vile situation instituted by Lenny. The miscreant had decided to adopt me early on to gain extra funds from the Welfare system, as well as he now could receive additional disability payments. He was fraudulent. There was no way out. I was just a child, and he could come after me at any time. I just prayed, and prayed, and prayed to God.

Living in Medford only escalated Lenny's psychosis. Eventually he became more reclusive, and his mental state actually deteriorated significantly. With so many ailments, he was not carousing with the other criminals of his ilk. Hibernating at home most of the time there were far more beatings inflicted on my mother. I remember one time, with a gun in his hand, he chased her from the kitchen, out of the back door, into the adjacent woods, and I heard a blast. It was one of the most frightful moments of my life. I had no idea if she would come back hurt; or we would find her lying dead amongst the dense trees after he had fired the pistol. Lenny either missed her or used the gun as a scare tactic. When she showed up at the house disheveled and hysterical, I could feel myself falling to the ground in despair. As usual, mom managed to bare the degradation and the pain inflicted by the monster. Again, I was in prayer, and this time I requested God to keep my mom alive. My fear and anxiety for my mom and siblings was increased by centillions.

The pain and suffering inflicted on my mother and brothers became more frequent as the days wore on. It seemed every day, if not twice a day, someone felt Lenny's fists. At other times Lenny randomly spoke of killing my mother. Many times, it did not appear to be a scare tactic. And, one time he almost succeeded. Grabbing mom by the head, he put it to the heating element on the gas stove and said he was going to have her burn. She yelled to her sister, Angie for help, who was watching the near catastrophe, to use the telephone and call the police. When Aunt Angie saw what was happening to her sister she went over to the phone on the wall and ripped the cords out. Mom's sister was a duplicitous character in the relationship between my mom and Lenny. Now, thinking back I know Lenny and Angie were both deranged. But this time mom was saved due to a malfunction of the stove burner. For an unknown reason, it was locked and did the flame did not ignite. At the time I knew God was watching over her. My heart and mind reasoned there could not have been any other intercession. Mom also believed it was one of the many times God was with her. Yes, she prayed and believed in God.

Finally, the abuse became so violent; my mom gained enough courage to leave *The House of Madness*. She evacuated all of us to a crisis shelter. However, this hopeful change did not last. The monster had heard from a relative where Mom was lodging and found her. I surmised he either threatened her or us kids or made promises of change in his actions I knew he would never keep. However, with no education, no job or skills, six children to feed and shelter, she gave in to Lenny, and we returned to the abusive house with the devil.

The chaos continued, but at least for a time, it was at a minimum. People may wonder why my mother let this happen to her for so long. But, unless one lives through an abusive relationship, it's hard to understand. I am confident he threatened to hurt their offspring if she tried to leave. The only positives in mom's life were her children. Although she didn't physically show us love, I know she did love us all very much. She would do anything she could to protect us from getting hurt. Although unable to keep Lenny from abusing her she did not want to make him angry enough where he would beat on or hurt her children.

During this time, I became increasingly attached to Hanna, Aunt Angie's child. She was the cutest baby with the most prominent brown eyes and beautiful, soft and curly light blond hair. I adored her and instantly took her on as my charge. It hurt me to know the circumstances created by her birth. When Hanna was little, she had no clue she belonged to Lenny. She was a smart, sweet and shy child but not talkative. I believe as she grew older, she was not oblivious to the strange relationship between her mother and Lenny. When she became of age, she apparently figured Lenny was her father, not the anonymous guy from Pennsauken who refused to acknowledge her birth. However, it was in her character to keep silent. And, this secret was not a topic to be discussed. I developed a close bond with this vulnerable child and have been forever devoted to her throughout the years.

My Aunt Louise, my dad's sister, and her daughter, Cousin Susan, who was four years younger than me, were both a strong support team in keeping me sane at different times during the chaos while I lived with

Lenny and my mom. I spent as much time as I was allowed at my paternal grandparents' home, where I was nurtured not only by them, but also by the entire extended Casford family. Violence, fiascos, and chaos were absent at the homes of my extended family. I am sure they are part of a team of Angels designated by God and my dad to protect me from the continuous struggles at *The House of Madness.*

Aunt Louise was consistent with questioning me regarding any molesting goings-on me by Lenny. Later in life, she told me my dad's brothers had threatened Lenny to make sure he did not lay a hand on me. Time after time, my dad's family tried to remove me from the evil-doer's house and have me live with them. My mother would not relent. I believe she needed me. Emotionally, I was the caretaker of her soul and the cord connecting her to the memory of my dad. Perhaps, mom always associated my presence with the love she had for my father. This rationale helped to keep her sane. I really never asked her.

Most of the families in our community of Medford appeared to have money. Our tribe did not. We were the epitome of the lower class. Lenny may have had money from his drug deals, Disability, and Welfare, but he did not spend it on my mother or us kids. He was always in the market for a new car and other material items for himself. Many times, I remember going with my mom at night to the Goodwill donation boxes to search for clothing. She would lift me up so I could reach in to pull out bags of other people's throw-offs.

When we reached home all of the kids rummaged through each bag as though it were Christmas. We all tried on clothing that fit or looked somewhat useful. On that note, Christmas was not an exciting time for my mom or the children in our family. Mom never received a gift from Lenny. A few small trinkets were thrown upon us, but not a lot. Thankfully, my Grandmother Leona bought presents for everyone and delivered these gifts to me while I waited outside the house. I was always so excited to meet her when she arrived by car, as she would never step foot inside the house. Her acts of love made the holidays a little better for all. We had food during the holidays but not much. During rare times, my friend Carene would come to visit, she was surprised to learn I had been in the cornfields stealing so all of us children could have something to eat. To this day she reminds me of this unusual foraging event.

Many school children in Medford made fun of me due to my skinny frame, my Goodwill attire, and the knowledge I appeared destitute. However, Lenny was not penniless when it came to cash. While around the house, he acted like how I thought a low-level Mafioso would. He usually wore muscle t-shirts to show off what he believed was a perfect body and acted as if he was one of the top-ranking bosses of the mob. The drama never ended with him.

When he traveled to secret places to meet his miscreant friends, he dressed in expensive clothing with all the spark and glamour of the wealthy gangsters he aspired to emulate. His accessories were always solid gold chains, other precious jewelry and diamond rings. As the years went by, he adorned his body with a myriad of tattoos. I think he thought of himself as a Goodfella. The lot he hung around with were surely gangsters, but at least they took care of their immediate families. Lenny did not. He took care of Lenny. Self-loving, selfish and with an incredibly high opinion of himself; he liked to think he had class. At the same time, he kept his family in poverty. Lenny's actions never gave credit to his one hundred percent Italian heritage. He was not a family man. He was merely a family destroyer. It was a sad time for me, as well as my siblings. No! He indeed was not a Goodfella.

The few times Carene's mom would allow her to visit while we lived in Medford. she never stayed long when the violent one was around. The girl was also well aware there was not much food lining the cupboards or in the refrigerator. Lenny ate out a great deal or made sure the available food was for his consumption. I usually went to the homes of the few friends I did have but never asked them to my house. Shame was an ever-present companion to me. Embarrassed for friends to meet my dysfunctional family, I never knew what would trigger a violent act from Lenny. Most of the friends were left at bay. This maneuver was more comfortable than sharing my family life and losing the few friendships I had made in Medford.

It was vital for me to be able to buy clothing for myself to fit in with my peers. I was not going to allow the Goodwill donation box to be my permanent boutique. When old enough while living in Medford, I took any job available to keep me away from home. And, it came when I had my first real job at McDonald's. It was great! Not only was I paid, I was also fed. Many times, at the end of my shift, I snuck food in my purse so I could bring home to my siblings. When I arrived with these small packages, it was like a holiday. My siblings were so excited. I considered it a responsibility to help my mom and care for the children.

I also began to save some money knowing I had big dreams to move out on my own. Many times, I ran away, committed to never return. Once, I had a friend drive me to his grandmother's in Philadelphia. Somehow, my mom found me, and brought me back to the hell hole. I loved her so much, but she continued her desire to keep me in prison with her. Yes, it was a veritable prison.

Well, my big dreams were shattered when I learned we were again moving, this time out of state. The new destination was Bedford, Virginia. Not only was it bad enough to have Aunt Angie's first illegitimate child, Hanna in what should have been my mother's house, but to make matters worse, Aunt Angie became pregnant again with a second child by Lenny. Jay would be the next progeny of the incestuous relationship. And, people in the neighborhood were still talking about Hanna. Again, Angie never left the house, did not have a boyfriend, or a job. Tongues were wagging in the community and not charitably.

Life became more complicated for our family during another significant development. The persistent detectives who were diligent in trying to solve the murder case in Camden came around again to interrogate Lenny. The monster could not take flight fast enough to get out of town. So again, he planned for a quick escape. Our family became skilled movers at packing up and fleeing. Lenny was determined to get us all as far away as possible to avoid the authorities, as well as, to avoid any further questions by ADF regarding Aunt Angie's new pregnancy. We were the most duplicitous family in town. Decent people knew us and kept a fair distance. I often wondered if they thought of us as trailer trash dwelling in a stick house.

Abuse

A fist to the head
A fist to the face
The never-ending torment for your faithful Grace
You made me believe you would comfort and care
But, in a split second, you changed
And, I forever have been frightened of you
My babies also fear your violence
And, they too cower to your abuse
You torment them as well
We all live in a house called hell
Someday it will end
I hope before I die
In your house of abuse, violence, and betrayal
I guess I will daily cry
But, eventually, I will run
Before you use a gun
And, that will be a blessed day

~Michele L. Shriver, Author

Chapter Twelve
The Strength of Grace

ALTHOUGH MANY MAY THINK MY mom, Grace, was not a caring person for her inability to show me much love; I believe her life was so chaotic, love was emotionally foreign to her. She was surviving in the only way she knew how. Just staying with this man, who brought so much fear, deception, violence and pain in our lives shows strength. As a child, my mom had lived a terrible existence. The house she lived in was often cold with little heat, and there was never enough food, but, usually a good supply of alcohol. But mom always had faith. Somehow, she kept a strong belief in God and apparently held to the wedding vows, "for better or worse." And, her life was undoubtedly the worse. The only time she knew real love was with my dad. Her fairytale life with him was tragically short-lived. I believe she was limited in giving love to her children. Her style of providing love was manifested in different and unconventional ways. With the few pennies she ever had to spare, she would take one of us to the store and allow us to choose our favorite snack. We had very little growing up, so this was a big deal. My siblings and I would argue as to who was going to accompany her on those rare outings.

I loved singing and dancing, and as a child always wanted to be famous. It does not take much imagination to wonder how I could aspire to such a career. Thank God for fantasizing. I would gather my sister and brothers and ask them to make up a dance with me and perform for my mom. She loved it when we made an effort to show off our amateur talents and always had a small smile as she patiently watched us. Perhaps taking the time to be our audience was her way of showing love. At times, I would dance solo. Seeing her sad smile as she watched my staged show made me want to continue to perform these little sessions of entertainment. During those theatrical moments I could tell she loved me in her own distant way. At other times, she put herself in danger when Lenny was mean or violent. Once in a great while, she did voice her opinion and tried to take our sides. When Lenny would not allow me to go to my grandmother's house, I would sit at the kitchen table and cry for hours hoping he would change his mind. My mom would try to reason with him, knowing she could be heading for another beating. The fear was always present, and fear was not only for herself but for her children's safety as well. Strangely, he did not subject me to the beatings he inflicted on mom or the other kids. As I said previously, Jenna had not been subjected to the actual beatings, except for the one-time Lenny pulled her up by her arm. I may have been privy to the tirades, and whippings; however, I endured other punishments for my sins. He would think nothing of clubbing one of his kids with his fist or consistently punish one of us to get back at mom. Perhaps this was one of the reasons she never left. Her leaving him could cause distress and abuse for one of us. I know now, as an adult, for all the years she lived with Lenny, she was a prisoner in an incredibly deep abyss and could not find her way out.

Book Eight

Chapter Thirteen
Lenny Runs the Herd to Virginia

IT WAS CONSIDERABLY MORE DISTRESSING for me to move from Medford, New Jersey to the State of Virginia compared to moving a short distance within the state. Relocating further away from my dad's family had me terribly anxious and frightened and those feelings were quickly escalating. I did not want to be hundreds of miles away from my real family's home. After all, dad's family was my safety net.

On the last day before the move, my Aunt Louise, my dad's sister, and her daughter, Cousin Susan and I had a plan. After the day ended Aunt Louise, would wait at the front door of the school and drive me to my Grandma Leona's home to live, forever. My mom must have overheard me talking on the telephone to my Cousin Susan and showed up at the school before the bell rang at the end of the day. I knew then my plan was futile. I cried and cried and now believe my mom needed me more than I needed her as a mother. I was her strength and the weight of this responsibility, taking care of a parent while still a child, forever loomed in my mind.

Although at the time I found her actions to be selfish, and caused me great sadness, her dependence on me was again her way to hold on to sanity and make some sense of her imperfect life. As the oldest, I was also a great help to her while she tried to raise my siblings. The constant presence of me in *The House of Madness* kept Mom's psyche tethered to the memory of the love she shared with my biological father. Without realizing her deep attachment to me, she had held me captive from the freedom I hoped to gain, and the healthy life I ventured to achieve living with my Grandmother Leona. She could not let go of me. I was again, and as always, a prisoner, in *The House of Madness*. As much as I adored and loved my mom, there was no way out. Invisible bars seemed to be permanently around me, and I always felt trapped like a caged pet; especially detrimental to the freedom of my soul and being. Again, in my own way, I began to pray. This time, more urgently for freedom.

I was sixteen years old when we moved to Bedford, in the state of Virginia, a town located smack in the middle of the Blue Ridge Mountains, beautiful but desolate. We had relocated so many times in my life, but always in the state of New Jersey where the people and cities were familiar to me.

Under different circumstances, and, possibly a more compliant attitude I may have been able to cope with the change; but this non-adventure was pretty much determined for a flight from the authorities. The outcome would be unpredictable. This erroneous get away was not for the betterment of our family. It was an escape from Lenny's reality.

With his persistent rants regarding the authorities pursuing him for the crimes he believed were not his fault, our family was herded southward like cattle moving from one pasture to another. He had assured himself this new territory was a great sanctuary for him to become invisible, or so he thought! We were finally in an area where people and neighbors hardly existed. He believed he had found his panacea.

Determined to relocate to an area as far away from civilization as possible, the man was too ignorant to realize the Vice, as well as the Homicide Squad would be resolute in their search. In the secluded and sparsely populated hollows of Virginia, it was actually easier to find him. He was not the proverbial "needle in a haystack." More recognizable due to his New Jersey accent amongst the dialect familiar to the people of the mountain enclave, he was more detectable than ever. Before the relocation, his reckless planned journey appeared to be the 'Great Escape'. But the authorities were relentless.

The miscreant was not half as smart as he thought. Investigators gained knowledge of the new location from an informer in Medford as to Lenny's whereabouts. To his dismay, the knock on the door catapulted him into a moment of panicked reality. However, as usual, the criminal once again had devised a plan. My mother had previously been cautioned by Lenny to lie to the authorities regarding any questions relating to the time frame of past crimes. The fear she internalized of her criminal husband was far greater than her fear of the police. When questioned she was a complicit partner in the knowledge of the recent murder in Medford, as well as a murder in Pennsauken. Taken in another room for questioning. mom gave Lenny the alibi's he needed; sparing him from the never-ending questions asked. Also, when questioned by *Children and Family*, who were also able to locate the dysfunctional bunch and daring not to go against Lenny for fear of vengeance she was duplicitous regarding Aunt Angie's last pregnancy. I am sure my mother was complicit with whatever story Lenny concocted to deny the incest. What else could she do? Mom was afraid of facing life, let alone her own life. She was entirely dependent on him for the meager dollars he spared and had no strength, power or support to live a life on her own. Merely a case of self-inflicted and self-destructive misfortune. My sadness for her simply deepened.

Bedford, Virginia was a far cry from the city streets of New Jersey. Developing new relationships was complicated. People here were clannish. To their ears, I had a strange vocabulary and talked much too fast for them to get the drift of my conversations. I was alienated from everyone I loved and cared about. And, surely to far from the city for my liking, and I was devastated to leave my dad's family where security and love were plentiful. For a strange transport, living in the typical environment for those who had made their home in these hills for generations, I was a peculiar figure in what was for me uncharted territory where I was imprisoned in a different way.

I especially missed my Cousin Susan, who had always shrouded me in a long-lasting spirit of love, and endless support. She was the rock I so needed in my constant battle for a healthy existence; a mental lifeboat in my spastic life. In the past, she could be counted on in a moment's notice to rescue me when circumstances became dire. The people in my dad's family were a significant source of strength and safeguarded me from my abnormal life. I had come so near to living with these good people before again being uprooted by Lenny and my mom. Now, I was lodged in an unfamiliar place with unfamiliar people. Most of my peers in the Virginia sticks thought I was weird. And, honestly, I did not know what to make of the mountain people. I just did not fit into the world of the Blue Ridge population. They talked differently, Southern, slow and steady and I was the new outsider, talking fast and furious. Like Dorothy in" The Wizard of Oz", I just knew tornadoes were coming, but when? I cried my heart out daily, not realizing, one day, I would shed infinite tears.

Our house in Virginia, I say house no more than a place of emotional and debilitated misfortune, stood in the middle of nowhere on a dirt road. There were mountains all around us. I felt I was in a gauntlet. The place was a brick raised ranch with a half-finished basement. One half was a garage. And, here again, Amy was lucky enough to live in one-half of the concrete enclosure. The garage half. The worst half! This time mom tried to make the dark, dank hovel look more like a room. She hung blankets on the walls, and garage door. Knowing I liked tigers she found a huge faux tapestry of a tiger and hung it up as well. All was accomplished with the hope it would feel warm and cozy. She used rugs to cover the raw, damp, and dingy concrete. Actually, all the decorating did not accomplish the warm and cozy feel. The garage was ice cold, and I was freezing. I believe my mom was so depressed, she simply managed to shut out the realities of a normal existence for me and herself and survived in the best way she could.

The other half of the garage was a heated room. It was designated as Aunt Angie's bedroom. Now, for me to get to the main floor, I had to go through her area and up the stairs to get to the only bathroom in the house. This was inconvenient, but it was better than when I had to go outside to cross the yard to get to the bathroom in the house; especially in snowy New Jersey winters. Later, Jenna was told to share the space in the garage with me. She was only nine years old at the time. Too little to have been told she should sleep in a dark, cold place, but it was her father's rule. Apparently, she was smarter than him. Jenna decided to occupy the living room couch each night. Luckily, not reprimanded for commandeering the area it made me feel so much better to know she would at least be warm.

Amid all the turmoil, I met a sweet, young guy, Harley, who became my new boyfriend. He attended the same high school. One time he visited me because I was so sick. I remember him saying, "Amy, we gotta get you out of here. You are ill and will freeze to death." Well, luckily, I did not get any sicker and, I did not freeze to death. In one way, I really didn't mind being in the garage. It was a place of solitude and escape from the people above, in *The House of Madness*. Most importantly, I was away from Lenny. Although my pretend bedroom reminded me of a meat locker, I spent a great deal of time there alone feeling comfortable in the silence. Lucky me!

While I attended school in Virginia, and halfway through my freshman year, I began to notice the real difference in the culture. Although people started to make an effort to be friendly, I did not have the same feelings towards the new community. Kids knew I was different by the way I spoke and many times I was called Yankee. Even Harley called me Yankee Tail. I attended a vocational school for half the day. Part of the day was a course in cosmetology. The other half-day was academics. I knew college was out of the question. My mom never talked to me about higher education. In cosmetology class, I had a handful of friends, primarily due to our mutual aesthetic interest.

Of course, I never allowed any of these friends to come to my house. It was an insane asylum. Lenny's moods became more peculiar and escalated to the point of severe paranoia, and I was totally embarrassed about living in the garage. Sometimes, on the weekends, there were sleepovers at the homes of the few friends I made. And, I was determined to stay away from the turmoil as much as possible. When I began to seriously date Harley, I regularly escaped to his home and lied to my mom saying I was sleeping at a girlfriend's house. As a full-fledged teen now, and able to concoct realistic sounding stories to escape from the myriad dysfunction of my family the lies served me well.

To a degree, the investigations did seize after the authorities had decided they had sufficiently interrogated the duplicitous family. Lenny's craziness slowed for a brief moment. He appeared to calm down in his new environment. My mother was not subject to as many beatings, and strangely his kids did not seem to be as afraid of him. I believe he was doing drugs as often as when we lived in Medford, but at least not the hard kind; although he was drinking quite a bit and taking prescription drugs for his mental illness. I tend to think the change made him a minute fraction better. The paranoia was still there, but it was sort of a quiet nuttiness. His behavior was marginally human rather than the normal chaotic rantings. But the scale could tip anytime. To me, for a tiny moment in time he became less of a monster.

Although the incestuous relationship between Aunt Angie and Lenny continued, the boys, my brothers, appeared to look up to him. They were a nefarious crew and perused stores and stole merchandise of interest for Lenny. These actions of thievery solicited attention from their father the boys never previously knew. Lenny's recognition of the boys was better than none. God only knows why! He allowed them to smoke and drink when they were very young. He also allowed them to have tattoos on their body and ear piercings. My belief is he no longer had his drug friends to hang out, and he turned my brothers into thieves so he could continue to buy drugs. It was so sad for me to watch these young boys taking the wrong path in life. And, eventually, they all rose to the worst occasion, included trips to jail.

While living in Virginia, Lenny introduced my mom to alcohol. Because of her upbringing and alcoholic parents, she had never taken liquor until we moved to the mountains. He would force her to drink a big bottle of cheap wine until she passed out. Mom was so tiny at five-foot-two and now only one-hundred and ten pounds; a slight amount of alcohol sent her into a blackout. She could have said, no! as Lenny forced her to imbibe. But at the point in her life, where physical escape was impossible, the exit into the alcoholic abyss of her mind may have been more gratifying place than her real tragic life.

Lenny always managed to have a devious plan for his own personal gratification. This deed to keep my mom inebriated would allow him to carry out whatever sexual acts he had conjured up for Aunt Angie. Perhaps my mom liked being oblivious to the continued rape of her sister. In some way, he nefariously managed to control, either by alcohol, thievery, or sex almost everyone in the house. Except for the conversations initiated by my uncles about leaving me alone, I could never figure out why he had not taken a chance to molest me, mainly since now we were so far away from my family. Not that I would ever allow him to touch me in such a way. I would have put up a fight. He could never win. Thankfully, I never had to deal with his sexual abuse. Perhaps my actions toward him would have been severely dangerous for him. Perhaps!

"A Step toward Freedom
You kept moving us away from our familiar places
To rid yourself of investigating eyes.
When you did this, I lost touch with familiar faces
And severed my happy family ties
As usual, it was all about you
There was nothing I could do
I had to learn to go along and struggle
to live in a place, I did not know
But my heart knew eventually I would find my own path
And, my life would be rid of you
You ruined our family with your maniacal ways
And, as long as I live, I'll remember the day
I left your prison to get away."

~Michele Shriver, Author

Book Nine

Chapter Fourteen
Life with Harley

I MET CEAIRA'S DAD, HARLEY PEYTON, in high school. We were in tenth grade. I hated the environment at my home in the hollows and I hated being in Virginia. I felt terrible for my mom. I knew she wanted me at the house with her, but I could not live in the tumultuous environment any longer. I began spending a lot of time at Harley's. His family was friendly to me. The more time I spent at Harley's, the less time spent at *The House of Madness.* I had an escape. Although his family also had issues, it was nothing compared to the bizarre troubles and atrocities at my turbulent house. And, it surely was a relief from sleeping in the freezing basement garage. Virginia's cold garage was worse than the stand-alone car shed in Medford.

My mom and stepfather did not like the idea of me spending so much time at my new boyfriend's house. They would come for me, and I reluctantly returned home with them until I could manipulate my way back. By the eleventh grade, I began to spend all my weekends at Harley's home. And we began to have sex. Mom had never talked to me about how to protect myself against pregnancy. We did not talk about a lot of things and, certainly, not sex.

I can remember the exact moment Ceaira was conceived. It was the night of our Junior Prom in late June of ninety-ninety. I wore a big fluffy, pink gown, borrowed from Harley's cousin. His grandfather, Patrick, let us use his Jeep for the night. We had a great time at the dance. On the way home, we decided to make a pit stop on a dirt road in the woods close to Harley's home. After petting for a while, we eventually had sex. It was not the most romantic or most comfortable lovemaking, especially while wearing a prom gown. I did not think anything at the time. After all, he did pull out. It was our usual method of prevention. I don't know why, it seemed to work for everyone else. Just one drop and guess what? Between the cumbersome gown and the awkward position, we embraced; I am sure this exercise led to the birth of our daughter, Ceaira.

Let me explain. Somewhat, at least for a totally uneducated young teenage girl, all seemed safe until six weeks later while at Harley's house, I had terrible cramps on my right side and felt nauseous. We called the doctor's office, and it was suggested we immediately go to the emergency room to rule out appendicitis. Of course, on arrival at the hospital, the first thing I did was call my mom. After multiple tests, including the doctor's order for a pregnancy test, Harley was invited into the room. Shocked and surprised, we learned we had made a baby. Time again, to pray! And, surely this action would definitely call for a whooping from Lenny. However, the miscreant never reacted to the event.

My mom was in the waiting room, and I asked the doctor not to mention the pregnancy to her. It was agreed. I would take on the task of telling her at a later date. At this moment, I knew my whole life was going to significantly change. While my mom was driving us home, I became terrified and could barely breathe. My mind was a jumble of issues and thoughts were spinning out of control. I was only a teenager, barely into my senior year of high school and worried about the reaction of my class-mates. Strangely enough, part of me, although nervous and frightened, was happy. This was my way of permanently leaving my mother's home. I knew Lenny would not want a pregnant stepdaughter anywhere in sight. Yes, this was good!

I then transferred to the new school Harley had been attending. No one there would know me. I did not need to hear gossip regarding the bump at my belly. Finally, after a few weeks I told my mom about the circumstances. Ironically, she did not put up a fight. I believe she resigned herself to accept my situation. She fostered no real obligation to continue to worry about me. Finally, my mom appeared to realize it was a way out for me; and I actually believe she finally thought it was a good idea. Here

I am following in her footsteps, getting pregnant and escaping my living conditions. Ironic! Unfortunately, there would be unforeseen problems lurking down the road.

The pregnancy wasn't planned, but indeed was the catalyst giving hope to a flight of freedom and liberation. It was apparent, Harley, and I would need to live together and take care of our child. He was as happy as me to take on this new experience. I could not wait to move out of my mother's house, forever, and considered my pregnancy a blessing. Now, not only did I have a real reason to escape the instability of my house, but I was sure the birth of a child would keep me from making bad choices. I was going to be a loving, conscientious mother and I fully embraced the idea of nurturing a newborn. I could raise and protect my child perfectly. I was convinced, this was such a novel idea I had. Or was it?

My song for life could have been "Looking for Love in all the Wrong Places." I always searched for love but until my daughter, Ceaira, was born, I never really knew love or felt the emotions of being loved. The love I had and still have for Ceaira was unconditional. I knew from the moment she was conceived I was going to give her all the nurturing, security, care, and notice I never had. She would want for nothing. But, Harley? He was another story. In my own way, I thought I did love him, but was never really sure, young love, I guess. He was a good person. My baby never lacked my attention nor his. Young people live in a fantasy world. And, I was Cinderella without the coach or slipper. He was no Prince Charming!

Harley's mom, Denise, who lived next door to Harley's grandfather affectionately called Poppa, was an addict and entirely irresponsible to care for him. His grandmother had died from cancer, so his Poppa raised him. He actually felt tremendous anger toward his mom and pretty much disowned her. Aunt Darla, Poppa's other daughter, also lived next door. She is a wonderful person and became a tremendous help to me after and Ceaira was born spending many hours days taking care of my baby allowing me to finish my academics. The family lived in little community surrounded by each other.

Harley was always against drinking alcohol and taking any type of recreational drugs. He was happy to live in the stable environment of his Poppa's home, considering both his mother Denise's and his stepfather had addiction problems. Her husband was an alcoholic. As is the normal, when dealing with addicts, they tend to be sweet people when sober or drug free and his mom provided this side of herself on occasion. She and his stepfather were both kind people when not in a state of addiction. But their problems were perpetual.

A few years after Harley and I ended our marriage, Ceaira was about seven, Denise, who once again continued abusing drugs at the time, crashed her car into someone's house and died instantly. She was a great person when she was sober, and she loved Ceaira very much. Harley swore he would never indulge in these types of addictions. It was odd, but not surprising if you think about it, when in the later years our child, Ceaira, indulged in drugs and I was reminded of Denise. They both appeared to have the same behavior. Does every family pass the gene? During those helpless times, I was in constant prayer for my daughter's recovery.

As his last year of high school approached Harley worked with the police department to help apprehend individuals who bought and sold drugs. He never drank at parties where we were invited. If he had the opportunity, he would have turned in his mother to the authorities. This led him to a short career as a corrections officer. He was really pleased when there was a conviction of violators.

My baby would never be raised in a *House of Madness*. Amy's child who I would name, Ceaira, was going to be nurtured in a loving, safe, and sane environment. I had a goal and was determined. Normal was not something I knew as a child, but I was sure I knew what normal was going to be for my baby. I moved in with Harley, and Poppa and continued my education.

We were getting ready for our baby girl to be born. For the first time in my life, I felt an overwhelming abundance of inner joy. I was in love with the thought of motherhood. My heart told me I had finally found the freedom and peace I had always prayed for. It was the most exciting time of my life. Or, so it seemed.

Before my baby girl breathed air, there were medical problems. The doctor knew, she was breached prior to the suggested time of delivery; and an appointment was made for a Caesarian Section. Another problem occurred during a subsequent office visit and sonogram. The cord was wrapped around the baby's neck. According to the gynecologist, there was no safe technique to turn the baby around by a routine delivery. To prevent any further complications, the doctor delivered my baby five weeks early. God was present. I was absolutely sure.

Young Adult

When you think you are an adult?
You haphazardly scurry about
With no clue of what could be
With no notion of what's about to come
Young adults determinedly plant feet
Determined to never retreat
Blasting full forward
In the complicated world of life
The young deny the idea of pain and
suffering
And, when it comes along
It's not a sunny dawn
to wake up to
However, the young ignore
There could be suffering behind a door
It sometimes visits with tragic news
Summoning a young adult to
cry and doubt
Although thoughts of pain can blind-side
the most mature of us
Young adults appear to ignore a crisis knocking.
Moving along stealthily opening every door
Without caution no matter the outcome
Striving to be an adult is not an easy feat
Even for young adults who will endlessly deny
or retreat from a potential disaster
Oh, to be young

~Michele Shriver, Author

Chapter Fifteen
My Lovely, Ceaira

C EAIRA RENE PEYTON WAS BORN on March 16, 1990. She was five pounds and four ounces at birth, the tiniest little infant, with a full head of dark hair and surely the most beautiful baby I had ever seen. When I first held her and looked into her eyes, I knew for the first time in my life the meaning of pure love. She would have my heart, and we were forever connected by love. My dearest friend, Carene who was then studying at a university in Atlanta, drove to be by my side when Ceaira was born. My daughter's godmother.

There were dreams and plans for Ceaira's life determined well before her birth. She was my greatest mission. In my soul and mind I had already created a perfect existence for my newborn. As an infant there were so times, I packed her in the car driving around to try to get her to sleep, but I didn't fret. She was my fragile little doll and my adoration for her never wavered.

My baby was the sweetest ever, curious, happy, loving, and my love for her never wavered. She constantly looked around her space to make sure she didn't miss any events. As she grew into a toddler Ceaira accumulated a multitude of family and friends around who loved her. I was thrilled she had all this love.

Her amazing, friendly, and joyful personality became apparent. She was never shy and would converse with anyone. She loved cuddling and we always hugged each other. I never wanted to be alone without her, and I made sure we were together as much and often as possible. I really never had the desire to leave her because I needed a break. Ceaira was the break, and the only break, I needed. Recently, a friend mentioned to me she always remembered Ceaira and I walking together holdings hands. It was always the way with her at any age. I believed people perceived and recognized us as one spirit, one entity.

When our little girl was two-years-old Harley and I decided to marry. We did so on a beautiful sunny day, in May of Ninety- Ninety- Two in the town of Bedford, Virginia. The sky above was filled with a clear, light blue brightness, and the days temperature increased into the seventies. Dogwood trees were just beginning to bloom their flowers, and the Poplars were a majestic backdrop in the rear rolling hills. Ironically, the scene appeared a real turn-of-the century wedding with the cemetery greeting the wedding party at the front door of the church. Looking across the long-gone residents the front door to Poppa's house was gladly visible; another place of refuge.

To me the event seemed primitive. None of the party or guests could have denied the persistent odor of cow manure emanating from across the side field; although, the beautiful horses walking in their "natural gait" around us were a pleasant diversion from the all to present farm odors. So close one could touch their noses. We only needed a horse-drawn carriage parked at the front façade of the small country church to take us back a century or so. The location was definitely in the boondock of Bedford County Virginia.

The wedding ceremony was minimal. It was pretty much, "I do, I do" and there we were, Harley, me and Ceaira, a licensed family. Although, the event was simple I adorned myself in a lovely poi de' sole straight gown with lace at the neck as well as long sleeves, puffed out at the shoulders. It fit tightly to my bodice and a big bow on my derriere was attached to a long train. I had really big hair, all of us girls did back then. It was the style in the Nineties. I am sure a few of the guests who were life-long locals believed my gown a little to city-sophisticated rather than country simple. But, since I was citified to begin with, I reminded myself it was my day, my moment, and I loved glam

Ceaira was the flower girl. She wore a beautiful crown of purple silk flowers. Her tiny gown was white like mine with little puffy sleeves. She was absolutely adorable and so excited for me to marry her daddy. Of course, too little to understand the etiquette of walking one -way down the church isle towards the altar behind the bridesmaids she, without a moment's hesitation walked up and down without a worry as to who she could or would bump into. The entirety of the guests laughed. Harley, looked extremely handsome in a black and white tuxedo, starched white shirt, purple tie, and spit-shine shoes. There were several groomsmen attending him. At the time, he had the popular mullet look hair cut going on, short on the sides and long in the back. I was impressed he took the time to look more citified.

I had two maids of Honor, unable to leave either by the wayside. Carene was my life-long friend, and Susan, my sweet and supportive cousin. My sister Jenna and another friend were maids. They were all attired in gowns of the color purple adorned with jewel necklines, lace and princess style bodices. Harley and I had very little money and, Carene, who had a Major in Interior Design at a University gathered all us girls and proceeded to help us create beautiful purple, and white silk flower bouquets. She had just finished her exams at college and came to my rescue a few days earlier before the wedding to help me with all the pre-nuptial festivities.

My dad's family, the Cosford's all traveled from New Jersey to Bedford to share in my joy. Dad's father, Grandpa Finne gave me away. Since my Grandmother Leona and grandfather did not leave home much it made me feel awfully special to have them attend.

Chapter Sixteen
A Threatening Illness

WHEN I FIRST MET HARLEY, he shared he had a heart problem. However, I was never led to believe it was a major medical issue. And, I did not learn how deadly his affliction was until it was too late. Hypertrophic Cardiomyopathy was a congenital disease he shared with many of his family members. It is rare and often fatal. Most people affected never know the danger and die instantly during or without warning, catastrophic heart attack. There have been a few cases where athletes were on the court or field when this horrible medical tragedy occurred. The left ventricle gets so tight and thick, the blood cannot pass through to the chambers. For Harley, it was hereditary. He carried the gene. Unfortunately, many members of his family left this world way too early in their lives. Harley's, dad and his twin brother both died while in their thirties from the same condition. Whenever I visited Harley's home, I felt saddened when the conversation continually reverted back to the loved family members no longer living or those waiting for a heart transplant.

Actually, the Peyton family had been part of a study conducted by the National Institute of Health ("NIH") in Bethesda, Maryland. Each member of the study was asked to volunteer to help find a cure for the deadly disease. Harley was lackadaisical in keeping his appointments with the study group. When we met, he hadn't been examined or tested for several years, and surely overlooked the importance to inform me of the potential dangers. The Institute was aggressive in requesting him to make an appointment, but he neglected to fulfill his commitment to helping. I was so young, and I really did not fully understand the disease. Actually, in the beginning, I was oblivious to the consequences to become pregnant by Harley.

When Ceaira was three years old, we were asked to bring her to the clinic. It was determined she had a fifty-fifty chance of inheriting her father's illness. Unsettling information, it had never occurred to me Ceaira's life could be in danger.

When I finally learned the urgent necessity to have Ceaira checked for the potential gene we immediately planned a trip to the NIH. Many tests were performed on both Harley and Ceaira. The Children's Center was available to families being studied, and we stayed at the hostel for several days. One of the tests performed was the removal of a piece of the leg muscle on her calf. This surgical procedure would determine whether or not and how severe her heart problem could or would be. When all the testing was completed, our little family sat down with the physicians and the news was not good. Ceaira did, in fact, have the gene, and heart condition. For some people, the muscle can grow very slowly, and at a point in time the thickness could stop developing. It would be necessary for our little family to return each year to determine if the muscle had thickened.

I was so saddened by the diagnosis of Ceaira's illness and privately took on my previous ritual of prayer to assure her condition would improve as she became older. I also worried, as Ceaira grew into maturity, she would be obliged to accept she had the same heart condition as her dad and how it could affect her future. Sadness for Harley and my little girl dominated my life all the time. He had to live with the guilt he passed on the disease to his precious child. Ceaira's dad was really good at covering up his feelings and always acted like it wasn't such a big deal. Assuredly, his insides were churning.

A Mother's Plea

God, please spare my child
from all this pain
What would this affliction gain?
I pray to you
She is such a little thing
I do not know what to do
Why was she born with a heart so frail?
Can you fix it?
To you, I implore
For this child, I do adore
I'll say it in one short verse
Please save her from this tragic curse
She is my moon, my love, my light
And only you can make this right.
Dear God!

~Michele Shriver, Author

Chapter Seventeen
A Mismatched City Girl & Country Boy

ARLEY AND HIS FRIENDS WERE into wheeling and racing on mudflats. He also loved to be with his buddies around campfires telling family tales and hunting stories. What a mismatched pair we were. He was filled with joy regarding Ceaira, but there were a multitude of problems surrounding our lives. The biggest, Ceaira's heart. We continued to live our lives with hope, and for the moment neglected the other issues surrounding us.

Young people are so oblivious to major problems. After all, anything could be fixed. Right? Over the next few years, with help from Poppa, we purchased a mobile home. Harley's family owned many pieces of property in the mountains. Without a doubt, we were going to live in what I envisioned as total seclusion. Although I was excited about living in a new home, I was not too happy about being confined between the deep hollows of the mountains in the Virginia backwoods. When my family moved to Virginia, I missed the sounds, sights and lights of the city, as well as the beaches. And I became forever obsessed about running back to civilization.

Joy was not an emotion I possessed living in isolation. Harley and I were too young. Many times, this man boy flirted with young girls. His immature actions left me feeling lonely and neglected. He was incapable of giving me the love, and emotional security I sorely needed, and fantasized about. Unfavorable thoughts were silently swimming its way through my miserable and desolate life. Living with Harley had become an ongoing struggle for me. I felt constantly depressed with the seclusion and, for me, unconventional lifestyle of the people who lived in the hollers and mountains of Appalachia. I could not see myself enjoying riding furiously in a Jeep through the mudflats with the folks who experienced this sport. Nor could I endure swimming in cold streams, as well as improving skills to catch fish with my hands or going to the local gun clubs to shoot skeet. Although at the time, Harley did not drink, I disdained inviting people over to our house who forever showed up with a pack of beer in hand.

I was so out of my element and believed I was living in a parallel universe. To live the mountain life is a beautiful and satisfying experience if it is one's preference. It was without a doubt not my style of living.

Obsessed, continuously with my attraction to the nuances within a city; I missed the music coming from street haunts and theaters, the daily sounds of people engaging in café shop conversation, and the clatter of footsteps scurrying back and forth on paved city streets. I had become rooted in an environment of dusty, unpaved rock and sand filled roads; as well as persistent smells from cow and other animals permeating the air, along with bugs and mosquitoes flourishing in abundance. I just couldn't!

I longed to see the visual displays of seasonal themes in department store windows and the streetlights all lit up in vibrant colors during the Christmas holidays. Easter egg hunts and Halloween costumes were pretty much ludicrous to the mountain folks. However, the most significant loss for me was the site of the ocean with calming summer breezes and the distinct smell of salty sea air. Although my life was dysfunctional as a child, I had been lucky enough to live in a place where the city and ocean met seamlessly.

Harley was a child of the remote hollows, forest and vast mountains of Appalachia, where he found joy and happiness in Mother Earth's natural environment. He loved hunting for deer, rabbit, possum and birds, as well as, sitting on the banks of lakes and ponds fishing and catching frogs. A little too primitive for me. And, unfortunately for our marriage; this city girl became one of the most miserable humans God created.

My core was empty and riddled with longing at the same time. If I continued to live in this environment, where many valued the surroundings as majestic, I would lose a part of me I had held on to for so long. The City! Amy was more inclined to find pleasure in flower shops, and flower street vendors, as well as the trees lining city Boulevards. I did not find pleasure in the flowers, trees, lakes, and rivers of Appalachia. I fantasized the mountains were the tallest buildings I longed for in the metropolitan area where I had lived; the rivers and lakes became the Atlantic Ocean I so dearly loved and beckoned to; and the trees and flowers were parkways in neighborhood communities near my dad's family in Pennsauken and Medford. I was *Alice*, but not in *Wonderland*. And, the city was beckoning me!

Life may have been so much easier if I could have identified with the slow jargon of the women of the country, and their rudimentary way of going about each day. Perhaps I could have survived the mountain life. I needed the soul of the city, with all its moods and proximity to the roar of the ocean with all of its boldness. In my soul, I was a city girl living on the edge of the Great Atlantic. In reality, I lived in a place so foreign to my understanding, I determined to find an escape route back to where I believed I belonged. I had to. This life was all wrong.

It did not take long for me to realize I did not have feelings for Harley. Perhaps I never had. When you are just a child, to try and act like an adult life does not always turn out the way you think. I was in love with love, not Harley. Although I tried to find a way to be in love with him, I ended up feeling nothing for him. He did give me my beautiful daughter and was grateful. And, he was a truly good soul but not a soulmate.

Early on, my fantasy of having a little family in a little home was a grand idea. I had always thought if I married and had a small family, I would genuinely find love. Apparently, I was disillusioned by the discovery of my own naïveté realizing I was still only a child.

Going

I am who I am
And this I know
To measure up to others is a no go
You won't like me a bit
And will undoubtedly have a fit
When I leave you behind
In this space of time
If I don't follow your path
I will honestly know your wrath
That is your problem
And this is a fact
I'm leaving this place, this way of life, I cannot conform
It is just not my idea of the norm
Thanks for the trip
At first, it was a good idea
But I'm giving it the slip
And, you will probably flip
Good luck to you, I'm on my way
So sorry, I could not be enticed to stay

~Michele Shriver, Author

Chapter Eighteen
Amy Runs Away

I BEGAN TO DISTANCE MYSELF FROM Harley. My friends became my escape, and I took full advantage of their companionship; eventually also frequenting lengthy trips visiting everyone I missed back in New Jersey. These excursions became a soul saving ritual. When I was up north in the city on the Eastern Seaboard I was thrilled and felt joy, and happily lodged myself with my dad's family for long periods. However, my conscience caught up with me. It was not fair to keep Ceaira away from her dad. Nor was it fair to me. With Ceaira as my sidekick my car became a two-way slingshot up and down the ninety-five corridor After much consternation with my inner self, I temporarily returned to Virginia with an exit plan.

Returning home, it didn't take long to become severely disillusioned daily with Harley's same old self personality and life in the backwoods of Virginia. I made up my mind. My intellect was now in control, emotions were set aside. Divorce was not waiting for an acknowledgment from Harley or anyone else. It was going to happen now, right now! For me, life with Harley in Virginia was uneventful and terminal. However, he was against divorce and monumentally disturbed having never considered I would leave him. He became extremely agitated when I had contacted an attorney. However, I was more aware than him, a long-term relationship between us would never work out. He was a good ole' country boy, and I was anything but a country girl.

I had been a city girl all my life and the noise and hullabaloo of the city and the architecture of the high buildings and paved streets allowed me to feel free and alive. It was the chaos I knew and loved. The relationship had reached its end. For Harley, the realization of divorce was a cause for doom. I was elated the make-believe fairy tale would end. There was nothing left for me in Virginia. Ceaira was still young. I believed it an excellent time to not create permanent damage to my child. My little girl was too small to understand my separation from her father. I would manage to see she visited him as often as possible. I thought it too unsettling should I wait for her to be older. Finally, he gave in, and we compromised as to how to handle our delicate little girl. Actually, we managed to remain civil to each other when she was about.

The End

I've tried, I've tried
But I've left you today
And' now on my way
I'm trekking down the mountainside
With my child in tow
To a world, I well know
Please don't be upset
I have simply pushed my button to reset
My life has been ordained by those I have met
But now I have the courage, and I'm on my way
Don't be sad
I don't want you to cry
And, always remember I did try

~Michele Shriver, Author

Book Ten

Chapter Nineteen
Here We Go Again, With Patrick

O N ONE OF MY TRIPS to New Jersey, I stopped to visit a friend in Maryland and met a guy named Patrick. I was about twenty-five at this time. He was kind enough, sweet, quiet and loyal. And, we communicated well with each other. Although, knowing he wasn't the one for me I visited him often. I was desperate for some kind of stability in my life, and I thought in time I would like him or maybe love him. I was constantly testing the waters.

Denial has always been a big part of my emotional history. So here I was, again, pursuing a relationship I thought would, could, should work. Still, "Looking for Love in all the Wrong Places"; always, in love with love. I needed it so badly. I would give it more time. Manipulation was also part of my baggage and I used every strategy possible to have a lasting relationship. It was my personal ongoing characteristic.

Before the divorce was final between Harley and me, I ventured to Maryland to visit Patrick more times than I should have. At least it was a wonderful escape from the Virginia backwoods. However, I knew taking Ceaira forever away from her dad would not work. He loved her too much. But a little denial helped me navigate this new relationship. Patrick's home was beginning to feel more and more like my home. He was a wonderful surrogate father to Ceaira, loved her and treated her dearly; however, I clearly understood Ceaira was physically too far away from her dad. Although I did not love Harley, I was not without empathy. We both loved her equally.

Oh, again the thought of love. The fantasies of being in love with love. Eventually, I talked Patrick into moving back to Virginia with me. Yes, I was manipulative! Not even I could believe I was returning to what I disdained: and gave up the obsession to venture to my ultimate destination, Pennsauken. The guilt regarding taking Ceaira away from her dad, as well as, the Virginia relatives who loved her was causing me torment. I loved my Virginia relatives. They were the kindest, most giving and gentle people. This troubled heart and soul consistently battled the losses for Ceaira. The decision had now become more about Ceaira then my wish to return to what I believe was my real home base on the Eastern Seaboard. The Northeast was just too far from Harley, and I thought Ceaira needed her daddy. And, most often, I was frightened Harley would sue for custody if I left again. I had taken his child out of state. And, I had become a single mother. I knew I was heading for trouble.

Patrick and I had been together for quite a while. I was desperate for a stable relationship. I just could not get over 'the family thing'. I had made another wrong move by introducing Patrick into my already complicated life. Although, he was great with Ceaira, I finally resolved to not being in love with him. No sparks! No stars! Patrick was simply Ceaira's and my caretaker, while I strategized and planned to try to figure out who I was and where I needed to be. This was unfair to Patrick; he was a great person. I just could not find in him the intense feelings I thought would unite us. And, Harley was distraught and "Mad as a Hatter" as I continued to live with Patrick.

My relationship with Patrick caused Harley constant stress. He believed he got even with me regarding my escape from him. After dating a girl, Selena, for a short time, Harley had her move in with him. I did not understand why he was angry. I believe he thought inviting someone to live with him would cause me to rethink the divorce. It made no sense to me, and, I could have cared less who moved in with him. Apparently, in his mind, he hoped this maneuver would get us back together.

Emotionally, I was out of the relationship for good, however, my sadness for Ceaira and her dad was real. We had traveled a rough journey with each other. But it was over. I constantly flip-flopped regarding the relationship with Patrick. He was safe. Perhaps, I would find happiness with him if I stuck it out longer, however, if the arrangement with him did not work out, I would find love elsewhere. Maybe? Of course, there is always the old saying, 'if I knew then what I know now', I would not have wasted so much time thinking another man so soon in my life after Harley could end in happiness. Trying to find a modicum of real desire with Patrick was also a constant challenge. As sweet and caring to Ceaira and me, I was bored to the nines.

My optimism always, love would reign supreme. But, like all lovesick fools, I had the hard lesson of learning to love myself first before I became infatuated with another man. The task took many years, a load of self-confidence and under strange circumstances. Patrick and I were together for seven years; however, as the years passed, I became more and more anxious to again escape.

Although I believe he loved me and took great care of Ceaira, I could not acclimate to Patrick's way of living. He smoked and lied about it. I hated cigarettes. He was into cars. Surely an uninterest for me. He was too reticent and lacked the motivation to challenge life and really did not excite my inner need for adventure. I was not going to sit in car garages watching someone repair vehicles, nor was I going to be happy venturing to car shows. And, the most unrewarding past time was his affinity for hunting in the woods. I had seen and been in pretty much the same situation last time. Not me! It was a humdrum relationship. Day in and day out was the same. The routine was so expected, one could anticipate each minute of each day. In the end, I knew I had to let Patrick go. But not before I decided to marry him, a significant, selfish act.

Harley was going to get a lawyer and have Ceaira taken away from me. So, Patrick and I had a quick ceremony at the courthouse. At the time, I believed it was the only way I could keep my child. Harley gave up on the custody battle when he knew about the marriage. As a lover, my passion with Patrick was mediocre. In my heart I considered him more a good friend, and I knew I was not being fair to him. He was sincerely a kind and good person; unfortunately, just not for me. I foresaw no magic, adventure or mutual longings in the life we would have together. I was again stuck, and knew I needed more.

One month after the marriage ceremony I petitioned for a divorce from Patrick and left him shortly after. It was a pointless gesture to hold him hostage to a marriage with no possibilities. I did it out of spite. Knowing a marriage would guarantee me custody of Ceaira. My specialty, the continuous art of manipulation. I did not consider myself nice, but, as usual I was on a mission; love, freedom, peace and security, and the white Pickett fence. I had to 'keep swimming'!

Actually, what I really needed to fill my soul was still a mystery to me. God had been talking in my ear. No, I did not always listen. My choices did not always venture a good outcome. I again asked God, Jesus to help me find myself. I knew I was asking a great deal from The Lord, who I knew had a full platter of requests from other people likely dealing with more significant problems. However, in my heart and mind I also knew at some point, God would come through; and I would find, peace, love, and happiness. The question was when?

Chapter Twenty
Amy Finds Peace in Lynchburg

A FRIEND, MEG ASKED ME TO room with her. She had found a great deal on a house we could share, and it was affordable. I was now determined to focus on only Ceaira, and myself. Men were off-limits. The idea of a roommate seemed safe. I said, yes, to Meg and my new life with Ceaira began. No more hanging on to a man for a modicum of imaginary love, peace and stability.

At the same time, I moved in with Meg, who loved Ceaira; I was also offered a full-time position as a makeup consultant for the Clinique Cosmetic Company. Now knowing I would have a stable financial situation; I was able to afford my portion of the rent and was tremendously excited to be independent. My heart knew I was on the right path to a healing spirit. This adventure was going to be great.

The house we lived in was in the town of Lynchburg, Virginia. A hoard of college kids lived next door. This was not good. Meg began to date one of the guys who lived in an adjacent apartment house. As the months moved on Meg was determined to set me up with one of her boyfriend's friends. I would always refuse the invitation. My plan was in permanent mental ink - living alone with Ceaira and grateful for steady employment, had become the solution for a path to stability, independence and happiness. It was a perfect situation for us.

All through the discord of my life, Ceaira was the one person who consistently brought me joy. I could count on her love, and I adored her.

She was developing into a beautiful, pleasant and personable child. No matter how sad I became, Ceaira could change my mood and make me smile. She sang and danced around the house. Our souls were so connected. She reminded me of myself when I was a child without all the heartache and dysfunction familiar to me. Her imagination was unfathomable. I remember one year when she was about five, I gave her a life-size Barbie Doll for Christmas. Before Ceaira left for school in the morning, Barbie was placed in the bay window of the living room, and as the school bus dropped her off after she would tell her friends to wave at her sister who was waiting for her. Unfortunately, attending school was not easy for my little girl. She had a learning disability and struggled with this difficulty for all her academic years.

We loved a lot of the same music, laughed in the same way and our voices resonated in the same timber. We also liked the same clothing. As she became older, this sometimes became a problem, when I precisely wanted to wear a particular outfit and learned Ceaira had checked the wardrobe before I did. For me, this was a small infraction. The love for my child was so pure, I rarely had any reason to chastise this beautiful, smiling, affectionate child who gave me more love then I had ever known.

I was determined to always make sure she had everything she needed. More often than not, she probably had more than any kid her age. I was diligent about her fitting in with her peers. History was not going to repeat itself. Ceaira would have beautiful clothes and her hair would always be well-coiffed. After all, I was a hairstylist and makeup artist. There would be no dumpster diving for my baby. I banked the promise early on for my special girl.

As a child, I never felt I fit in. I suppose, I spoiled Ceaira, but I believe I taught her upright, moral values. She knew she should never discriminate against anyone if they didn't fit in. This characteristic naturally became part of her personality. Ceaira did not care if her friends were rich, poor, black or white: or different in any other way. The gift of acceptance was part of her evolving nature. She understood the meaning of the lesson to accept people for themselves, never opposing me on the value of others.

Chapter Twenty-One
Matt. Maybe the One

ONE NIGHT AFTER I HAD finished work, I picked up Ceaira from Harley's house. When I arrived home, Meg said she had friends coming over for the evening. I said, "It's fine," and thought nothing of her plan. I went upstairs to read a story to Ceaira and kissed my little girl goodnight before bed. When I came back down, I noticed Meg and her boyfriend and another guy. She then introduced me to Matt Florio. The three were playing cards and asked me to join them. Matt was very handsome and well built. Meg had a plan. She knew if she had brought someone over to play cards, it would not look like she was trying to set me up. He appeared a nice enough guy. I did not have a moment of sparks flying above my head. If anything, I thought he would make a lovely friend to eventually know. After Matt left, I did not think of him.

As the weeks rallied on, Meg's potential candidate for me to love, and be loved came around quite often with Meg's boyfriend. Eventually, he asked me the question, "Would you like to go out on a date?" I immediately said, "I have plans for the weekend." He did not give up. Knowing I liked to dance, one evening he showed up at the apartment and presented me with flowers. He asked if he could take me to a nearby club. I thought the gesture was sweet. His knee was wrapped in a bandage from an injury he received during a track meet. With flowers in his hand, and, his knee obviously hurt, I felt compelled to give this guy a chance. After all, he went through all the motions with a battered knee. Perhaps, I should let down my guard for a change. I knew he was really not able to dance, and Ceaira was safe this weekend with her dad. So, I said yes.

As time progressed with Matt in my life, I began to believe the relationship would be a stable, fulfilling, exciting and; perhaps, loving courtship with a person who had similar values as mine. Here, again, now in my third relationship, there were no fireworks. I eventually, however, guardedly held high hopes I would fall in love with him. He appeared to be a great guy. If I was going to have a relationship, all the checks and balances needed to be in place. My head told me it takes time to fall in love with the right person. Looking back now, I know he probably was not the right one either; but I did not realize this at the time of our introduction, or dating. It just appeared he was attentive and caring. I let my guard down and I would pay. And, I did!

Weeks went by, and I learned more about Matt, he appeared to have all the right characteristics and goals I needed to sustain a purposeful relationship. Attending college in Lynchburg, Virginia he hoped to acquire a master's degree in Science. During this period, he was not sure if he wanted to choose a career in sports medicine or another area in the same desired field of science.

Matt was from a small town in Connecticut, close to the beaches. He had an identical twin brother, and his parents worked at the pharmaceutical company, Pfizer. It appeared he had a good childhood and a great family. Everything I never had. After learning about all the fantastic attributes Matt and his family members seemed to possess, I was feeling terribly embarrassed about my dysfunctional, chaotic, deranged family.

It was during this uplifting time for me with Matt, I became aware my abnormal family was again on the run. The police were diligently on Lenny's tail. Apparently, he was still a suspect in the murder of another guy back in New Jersey. Through his criminal contacts, he learned law enforcement, again, were about to continue with their previous interrogation. Surprisingly, an informant actually knew of Lenny's whereabouts during the last and earlier unsolved murders. And, to his misfortune, with Aunt Angie's second child in tow ADC apparently was also not as lame-brained as Lennie had thought. Investigating where and who the father, or fathers were of these two children appeared to be on their timetable. Obviously, these scoundrels should be paying child support. Who should be paying child support? Oh, Boy! Trouble was closing in on Lenny's door. The small mountain area was rampant with the gossip regarding these two repugnant people. This time there was definitely no boyfriend or husband in site. The neighbors were highly suspicious. The good news was the family was high tailing it to another state. This time, Iowa. was Fine by me! No explanation necessary! I had a reprieve! My mental state would become much healthier without my strange relatives around, and I would not need to evade the question when Matt asked if he could meet my family. They would be gone by the time he became more interested in me. Phew!

This new man in my life had all the qualities of a great guy, but I felt something was missing. In my mind, I could not justify my negative thoughts regarding this seemingly awesome person. However, there were signs and time would prove so. I wanted to love him.

The first red flag realized by me was this man's obsession with his fitness. He seemed to think and spend too much time and energy on the condition of his physique. I began thinking it was me placing too much importance on his desire to keep fit. Many women prefer a guy who takes care of their body and presents well. Could I have been overthinking? He did have an interest in sports and science. I, on the other hand, was getting a different take on his preoccupation with his body.

Perhaps he needed to mature. I would give him time. Later I would learn about the characteristics of an indefatigable, motivated person. As we became closer, he began to act differently. I agonized over this fixation he had with his body image. The challenge was on. I had to determine if I was too picky in my choice of men; or in reality had I once again denied all the weak points in the character of an individual? And eventually, had I learned this fact to late in the relationship? I had to face reality. However, it took a great deal of time, even years, and a high level of irritability on my part to recognize the effect Matt's body addiction had on me.

Over time, Matt and I began to spend more and more time together. Ceaira liked him but was also a little jealous. She loved our exclusive relationship and was not immediately happy with the interference of another person. In her little mind, Matt and I were spending too much time together and not enough time with her. Even my roommate Meg, who was responsible for bringing Matt and I together, took offense and was terribly upset when he was always at our apartment. She had broken up with her boyfriend and now wanted me to be available for her to engage in activities for single people. I was really beginning to like Matt, or so I thought.

Comfortable with his coming around and his ever so constant attention to me, I languished in the apparent normality of his way of treating me, and consistent dependability. Eventually, Ceaira warmed up to him and seemed happy for his attention as well. We were together more than not, and we appeared compatible. The decision was made. It was time to move in with each other, and we did so into a house just a street away. While living in our new place, Matt continued his education. I was still working for Clinique. It was about a year later, while I was away on a business trip, I learned Matt planned to ask me to marry him.

He and Ceaira embarked on an adventure to look for an engagement ring while I was away. When I returned from my trip, he surprised me by getting down on one knee and asked the big question. Ceaira had been in her bedroom. I will never forget seeing her little feet at the door waiting with anticipation to hear my answer. How could I say no? He was a great guy. Ceaira loved him and became infatuated with the idea of having a second daddy. Of course, I said, yes, I would marry him.

I could not help thinking about the good life Ceaira and I would have with Matt. Knowing a great job for him was soon to be locked down was advantageous to the lifestyle we both hoped to achieve. Finally, I was going to be assured what I did not have previously as a child, a "traditional" family. My idea of perfection! This new life had always dreamed precious, exciting and stable was on the horizon.

Matt and I discussed what the plans were regarding his career. Would he continue looking for a position aligned with his love for science? The degree was nearly in sight, and this assertive and aggressive man was adamant about securing a place in a scientific field. He certainly had no intention to continue his job as a bartender. Success was in reach. Matt had big plans. We lived in the house we rented until Matt finished college. Financially secure, this fact alone meant everything to me. My dream of a stable family life was being fulfilled. So, I thought!

Lifestyle changed rapidly for Matt and me. Both of his parents worked at Pfizer in Connecticut. He now had an opportunity to work there as well. Immediately after applying, he was offered a position. The salary was excellent. We would have enormous financial stability. It appeared a good move. My only concern at this time was taking Ceaira so far away from her father.

Events in the cycle of life are unpredictable. If I had known then her dad was not going to live a long life, I don't believe I would have left Virginia. Harley was evidently not happy about me taking Ceaira away. However, we came up with a plan where she visited her dad on holidays and in the summertime.

While Matt and I were still living in Virginia, Lenny moved my mom and all the siblings to Sioux City, Iowa, where many of Lenny's family was now established. However, without my mother's knowledge the devious Lenny, and my Aunt Angie had a devious plan. They did something so wrong and evil, to this day, my heart breaks when I think of their scam. However, looking back at the event, as treacherous as it was at the time, it unexpectedly, and ultimately changed the course of my mother's life. I will never forget the morning my mom called from Iowa hysterically unloading her devastating situation on me.

Before mom left Virginia with Lenny, she worked many years for an elderly lady, Eleanor. Mom was only allowed to work since Lenny knew her. She was an old lady who would not threaten him. And, he pocketed the money mom earned. Mom visited her charge for about five hours a day to keep the woman company and accomplish a few chores. I met Eleanor once or twice. She had no family and became attached to my mom. Eleanor was not an ideal person to work for. She was quite demanding of my mom. Although the woman was a tough old lady, Eleanor and Mom developed a close friendship, and it gave Mom a way to escape the dysfunction of her home. I believe the old woman was aware my mom had a tough life; however, I am sure she did not know how bad, including my mom's constant physical abuse from Lenny.

When she arrived at the lady's home to check on her one morning mom found Eleanor had passed away during the night. Apparently, she had died in her sleep. I remember how sad my mom was about the woman's passing. She was the only real friend in her life. She must have loved my mom. In Eleanor's Last Will and Testament, she left most of her money to her.

It was not too long after Eleanor's passing, when the family moved to Iowa. A portion of the money mom inherited was initially for a down payment on the house she and Lenny had planned to buy. They indeed placed a down payment on a lovely home with mom's inheritance, as well as some nice furnishings. However, although mom was elated with her new surroundings, it didn't take long for happiness to slip into misery. She prayed to God every day to be free from Lenny and told God she would give up the house and all the material objects to be free from the despicable creature.

Time passed slowly in Sioux City, and after a few months, mom developed pneumonia and was hospitalized. And again, Lenny managed to abuse my mother. This time with malicious abandonment. While mom lay in a hospital bed, he had made up lies regarding her mental health, persuading the doctor to have her evaluated for psychological instability. This led to a more extended hospital stay and gave the miscreant, Lenny, the time to initiate a devilish plan.

During the night, before mom was discharged Lenny and Aunt Angie had taken their son, Jason and left all the other kids alone in the house; including thirteen-year-old Hanna who refused to go with them for another destination. Thrown on Hanna's bedroom floor was a note stating they had decided to move away together. The two culprits fled Iowa with all the money my mom was willed, including the funds to finalize the payment on the new house where they had planned to live. The papers were scheduled to be signed in a few days. It never happened, and unfortunately, the bank account was in both their names. Once he had the cash, he sent most of it for safe keeping to his sister, Beatrice, who lived in New Jersey

I received the heartbreaking call from my mom the next morning when she returned from the hospital. Learning from Hanna of Lenny's vicious departure mom was devastated. The house was empty, except for Aunt Angie's daughter Hanna, and the other children who refused to leave with them. Hearing her voice on the phone saddened and angered me. Although she had no love for the creature, she was dependent on him for at least a roof over her head. Overwhelmed, she did not know how to function. Lenny had always controlled the money, and she now had to figure out how to pay bills, feed the children, and take care of other household essentials. She lived in the house as long as she could with donations from the local church as well as many treks to food banks. Sadly, she managed all this with no electricity.

Ironically, in the coming months, we learned Beatrice was in the habit of spending most of the money on material objects for herself. Lenny, the ignoramus, was never able to enjoy the money he stole from my mother. If you want to call it Karma, it was the best. Someone with the same character flaws as him, who he thought he could trust, just stole my mother's assets as he had done. We then learned Lenny and Aunt Angie moved back to Virginia to a different area far from where they previously lived.

After all the years Lenny had tormented, and abused my mother, his immediate action, although a common trait for someone of his character, was ever more devastating. A human being so cruel and negligent he had not left one penny for my mother to support his brood.

Charlie Casford

*Mom and Dad's wedding
1972*

*Me, Mom, and Dad
1971*

For the little time he was here on earth he showed me so much love

Dad painting the new house

Mom helping getting our new home ready

*Mom Loving her Christmas
gift from Dad*

*Amy praying before
she could even talk*

Mom doing the best she can to smile after Dad passed away

A young Mom doing the best she can

*Ceaira was always
connected to me*

Harley and Amy's wedding

Ceaira age 2

Amy and Ceaira were like one

Ceaira was always posing

Ceaira's life-size Barbie; she acted like it was her sister

Ceaira loved cheering

Ceaira was in charge of her class pet

Our Angel, she left us so many great memories

Ceaira and her Grandmom Grace

*Halloween was
one of our favorite
holidays*

*Our Shining
Star*

Dancing the night away at Carene's
wedding at the Keys

Always giving her love

Chapter Twenty-Two
Grace Finds Her Way

THOUGHT IF I COULD TAKE Hanna from her, there would be one less child for her to care for. After a long conversation with mom regarding the child I talked to Matt, and he agreed to take the young girl into our home. He knew how I was regularly stressed by the tumultuous life my mother and siblings led. By then I had finally conversed with Matt regarding my deranged family.

We rushed to purchase a bus ticket for the young girl who arrived in Virginia with one suitcase. When the forlorn Hana departed the bus, I was immensely sad by the way she looked. Hanna was dressed in all black and seemed pathetically ghost-like. The white paleness of her skin was a sickening contrast to her black clothing. The chaotic living circumstances had taken a toll on the sad girl. Her personality and demeanor were so unlike the shy, sweet girl I knew the previous summer. It had been almost a year since I had last seen Hanna and she had gone dark. Totally dark! Gothic dark!

At the time of this crisis, Matt and I were preparing to relocate to Connecticut where he would begin his new job at Pfizer. I was more than elated Matt agreed with me to have Hanna live with us; and will always be grateful to him for his compassion to take on the responsibility. In no time Hanna was back to her old smiling sweet self. And, Ceaira was beyond happy to see her and have a girl companion in the house with her. Matt and I worked diligently to gain custody of this child. Eventually,

Aunt Angie, Hanna's mother, gave up all rights to her. Although, Hanna and I are ten years apart, we were always like sisters. I loved her. We have been through many horrible moments together but still remained close. I am so happy I was able to show her what a somewhat healthy, safe life could be. Only the Lord knows what would have happened to this shy, sweet girl.

Ironically, Lenny left the van for my mom. One cannot rationalize Lenny's actions. He was totally mercurial. With courage I never knew she had, and finally a modicum of freedom, mom gathered all the kids into the vehicle and drove to a new destination, Montana. For mom, I believe it was a test of faith and a turned fate. I was happy the scoundrel was out of her life, but she was destitute. Although her circumstances were traumatic, with Lenny now hundreds of miles away mom actually gathered the courage to align with her new independence. Though the unexpected deviousness of Lenny's abandonment left her penniless; she gained a self-confidence she hadn't known since my dad passed away all those many years ago. It was her time to excel.

Lenny had kept her a prisoner shackled with fear for all the years she had spent with her depraved husband. She would have never left this man while with him. She had tried it before with sad results. Untethered, his devious actions actually allowed my mom to find a strong spirit within herself she never knew existed.

When she arrived in Montana, mom found a place in the woods and with the kids put up a tent, and the down-and-out brood had a make-shift home. Finally, after all the years of suffering the egregious acts of the tyrant this abandoned, courageous woman and her kids found work at a nearby carnival. The lowly job was to prompt people to throw a ball in some sort of basket. If a person could accomplish this, they would then win a prize. When not at work the family found food at another food bank. Mom and the kids saved enough money, and with this courageous woman at the wheel, the uplifted and spirited new lady drove her brood back to Virginia. Larry, my oldest brother, stayed behind. For a short time, when she returned to Virginia, her children were able to stay with friends.

Although mom's independence afforded her to challenge her new freedom, I was in disbelief regarding her situation; and the brutes actions continued to leave me shrouded in anger. Ironically, crazy Lenny learned while in Montana, his family had lived in a tent in the woods. He, like many abusers, had a moment of conscious. Shortly after she returned, in a strange moment of compassion, he sent mom five-thousand dollars. The act was so unexpected. I determined, he may have thought if mom went to Welfare, the police would be on his tail again. I believe it was most likely his strategy to keep himself ahead of the authorities.

Mom became more self-sufficient than she ever imagined. With her limited education, and the traumatizing events surrounding her and my siblings, she was able to find a job at a Blimpie's sub shop. With Lenny's cash and income, she rented a small place for herself and the children.

However, her life again changed dramatically. My brother Larry, the oldest, who had stayed back in Montana, called mom and told her he had found a church community where he was supported emotionally and spiritually. Stealthily, and with God powering her, she gathered her brood and again moved back to Montana.

The state is where and when she met Isaac, who later became her third husband. He was a member of the church, and she came to believe he was the right person with a spiritual and moral standing. If her convictions were correct, they would together live her idea of a devoted and prayerful, Christian life. As a family, the crew moved to many different states and cities: Connecticut, back to Montana, Texas, then back to Virginia; and, finally, Tennessee, where she has now lived for many years with Isaac and a few of my siblings.

Matt's parents were retired and had permanently relocated to Florida. They planned to sell the family home they owned in Pawcatuck, Connecticut, a very cute ranch-style with a big beautiful yard and small serene pond. His parents agreed to let us live in their house and pay rent.

Finally, we moved to Connecticut on the East Coast of New England, where a little city and a lot of ocean greeted Matt, Ceaira and me. My little girl was in fourth grade and nine and a half years old. Once we were settled into our new environment; I had the realization my brain was beginning to conjure up unsettling thoughts regarding my precious child leaving me to embark on future trips and long summer vacations to her dad's, and the Peyton's in Virginia. Although sad at these thoughts, I was adamant regarding Ceaira's connection with her extended family and refused to allow her to become an estranged child to her roots as I had been. I wanted Ceaira to know her father and be a part of all her Virginia relatives.

Throughout the following years while living in Connecticut when Ceaira visited her dad, it usually took about two weeks after she stayed when I received numerous calls from my daughter. She sobbed, missed me and wanted to come home. And, I felt the same. I think we loved each other too much. Could a mother love a child too much? Could a child love a mother too much? I knew I was over-protective regarding her heart condition. I knew, I doted. We both knew each of us did not do very well when we were apart for too long. No matter what was going on in my life, while Ceaira was growing up, she was either attached to my hip or hand. It was the way I liked it, and so did she. Never did I feel I needed an out or time away from my child. She was my "blessing" from God.

My daughter had so many friends when she was young, but it wasn't until we moved to Connecticut where she met a friend for life named Maya. They were indeed like sisters, just like Carene and me. She and Maya had the same personalities, both fun and outgoing. Ceaira started cheerleading with Maya at school. This sport was part of her life through-out grade, school as well as high school. No one knew of her heart condition. She didn't act differently than anyone else. Only the act of running was a problem for her, and fortunately, this was not part of the cheerleading program. She certainly was not limited to the field of boyfriends. A reasonably pretty teenager, and for the most part a good girl, she had the guy's attention and knew it, breaking a few hearts along the way.

As Ceaira became older, she managed to have a beautiful soul as well as a dynamite personality. Her hair was long, dark and straight, and she had the most enormous green eyes. There were no siblings to interfere in my time with her. I had always been one of Ceaira's playmates, and with time, I became one of her closest friends. Ceaira had a learning disability always interfering with her schooling. School was a significant challenge for her. However, she had a fabulous social life and was always surrounded by friends. This was the part of the school she loved.

I was a young mother, and we were sometimes like sisters fighting over silly things, especially borrowing clothes. This became the norm. I liked young-looking clothing. At times it was fun to share, but at other times hard. I guess knowing when to draw the line was the real trick with a strong-willed teen, but she knew when I meant business. Somehow, with difficulty, I managed to be the mom more often than being a friend. Ceaira pretty much told me everything happening in her daily life until she became older. It is a difficult period when a child no longer enjoys conversations with her parents. I suppose this is a sign of independence. When asked, I usually gave her reasonably good advice based on my own experiences. Sometimes she would listen, sometimes not. We were so alike in many ways and strangely had the same tone in our voices and silly laugh.

One time, when she was eighteen, we were shopping at the mall and eating ice cream, and the cashier asked if we were twins. Ceaira's reply was, "Oh, my God, No! This is my mom." She was monumentally annoyed someone would think we were sisters. I was so elated, I told everyone I knew of the experience. I identified with her in so many ways. Ceaira will always be my first love. All in all, it was the best relationship.

Getting back to the relocation from Virginia to Connecticut; I was elated to be in the region of the North East I so loved. The ocean was like a magnet for me. Sitting on the beach with the salty air blowing in my face granted me a calmness I so desperately needed. If I could have, I would have swallowed the saltiness to ensure the inner peace lasted for eternity. However, again the underlying feelings of unease reared its head. Trying to stay busy fixing and decorating the house, to make it more suitable for our lifestyle, was somewhat of a diversion from the steering's in the pit of my stomach. We were settling in and it was now time to concentrate on plans for our wedding. Perhaps I had the marriage jitters. Really? I was so busy with all I had to handle. And, vowed to push my worries to the back recesses of my brain. The wedding would be perfect. The house would be lovely. We both had good jobs. Everything appeared to be great. Matt grew up in this house, and I knew it was dear to him. He seemed so happy in the familiar surroundings.

My best friend Carene came to visit, and seemed pleased with Matt as my future husband, and appeared utterly happy regarding our new life together. My dad's family in New Jersey had met Matt a few times. They enjoyed his company and looked forward to another visit with us. I was finally getting excited about the wedding. And, Matt was totally thrilled we would surely be a married couple.

Thankfully, Matt's parents paid for most of the arrangements. They were well-off and incredibly generous and supportive. His mother was tremendously gracious in helping to plan the event, and I was so happy for her involvement.

We were married on August 19, 2001, in the little village of Watch Hill, Rhode Island. It was the most beautiful wedding I could have ever hoped for. The church was directly across from the *Ocean House,* rated one of the most prestigious hotels in the country. Watch Hill is a well-to-do community by the expansive Atlantic Ocean. where velvety sands sparkle; and stately mansions line parkways. The sun shone brilliantly on the memorable day, and many photographs were taken with the Ocean as a backdrop. and although a little on the hot side, I was finally feeling happy beyond expectation. Luckily, the festivities held at the Watch Hill Inn turned out perfectly. The reception room was decorated in all white lights. There was a two-hour open bar. On each table were vases filled with lavender and white flowers; and a DJ played all the music current at the time. The occasion surely was a whole lot different from my marriage to Harley. A tiara crown of seed pearls and zircons attached to an English silk tulle floor length veil sat on my head. I was lucky to be adorned in a beautiful princess style, silk gown with enormous fluffy ruffles below the waist. The bodice was tight and flattering, with Alencon Lace sleeves. Matt looked so debonair in a black tuxedo, crisp white shirt, with a tie to match the lavender color of the bridesmaid gowns. Carene, my Maid of Honor, Susan, and Hanna were all dressed in simple, elegant lilac gowns. And, of course Ceaira was the mini star of the bridal party with her tiara matching mine. She was happy and delightful. The surroundings were completely juxtaposed to my wedding in Virginia with Harley where the cows mooed while we said our vows.

And, with my real dad's family present it became one of the most joyous, and significant times of my life. And, the beast was not there to bully me or the other close relatives. Yes! it was a joyous occasion. And, yes, I felt like a princess.

Matt and I embarked on a cruise for our honeymoon. We decided to get pregnant right away. Thinking it would take up to a year, we were happily surprised when it happened sooner than expected. The ambiance on the cruise appeared to help us become a real family. I remember in September I was shopping in the mall for a birthday gift for Matt and felt sick. This prompted me to visit the pharmacy and purchase a pregnancy test. I skipped to the restroom and immediately conducted the test and was a little stunned. Baby! I wrapped the results up for Matt's birthday and gave the present to him. We were both so elated.

The stress from preparing for the wedding had finally abated, and we could live a pleasant, relaxed life in an area where we both loved the weather and the closeness of the city and beaches. After all the misgivings regarding the marriage to Matt, and my stress to commit I regained a modicum of joy and peace and believed this new life would be great. I now had a loving husband, and a beautiful family. Also included in the family, Hanna joyful, and independent found a job at a local grocery store. And, I acquired a position at Macy's department store as a makeup consultant. Outwardly, life appeared to be going along very well. I, again, began to feel some hope for a stable future. Possibly?

On May Sixteenth, Two-Thousand-Two, Jesse Matthew Flori came into our world; however, before birth, there were some complications with our son. The doctors told me there was an eighty-five percent chance he would be born with down syndrome. An amino acid test was immediately performed. It took one week for the results. I consistently prayed for my baby to be healthy. Even though I had not been to church since I was a little girl, I knew there was a God and always asked him to intercede during my daily personal and family trials. And, always believed God was part of me. Now, more than ever, I needed him. Matt accompanied me to his church, and I prayed and prayed. God must have heard me. The test came back negative. "He" did not forget about me. I just sometimes forgot he is was my best friend, and had always been there when I needed him, even when I forgot about him.

Eventually, we purchased Matt's family home from his parents and started to make some real changes to the décor favoring our lifestyle. Because childcare was so expensive, we decided I would be a stay-at-home mom with the kids. I was able to secure a job babysitting at our home for a teacher who had a child the same age as Jesse. I loved taking care of children, and the extra money helped.

But again, something was wrong. Why I had these feelings deluded me. Finally, I had a home, family, my children. But! There was an emptiness in my soul burgeoning to haunt me. I felt terribly unhappy thinking perhaps having another baby would help. The adoration for my children was the greatest love I ever had. I had convinced myself this idea would be the best solution regarding these nagging feelings of distress. I would be fulfilled by having a new baby and add more zest to my life. For a few years after Jesse was born, we tried to get pregnant but were not lucky. It was extremely upsetting to me not being able to conceive. In the end, it was probably God's way of keeping me from making another serious mistake. Adding another child to our family was surely not going to resolve my anxieties. And, the delusion began early. Those marriage vows, "for better or worse." How does the Bible define worse? I am not going there, but I believe different faiths define the vows differently. I now imagined 'worse' meant doom.

The failing marriage of Matt and me became evident when he launched a new project for himself to work out, and with extreme intent my husband focused on his body image, health and the condition of his body. He consistently challenged himself to grow strong and develop a healthy physique. When Jesse was four years old, Matt decided he wanted to compete in bodybuilding and set in motion a plan for this new endeavor. His demeanor changed and family came second to the new hobby. It was apparent Matt dedicated most of his time to the new adventure. A road to self-fulfillment! He could always follow through on any aspired pursuit, and this was no different. He commenced to work out often and religiously. However, this continuous assault on his body took a toll on his mental health. Although his body was looking fantastic for a weight builder, he was hard to live with.

Each day he allowed himself only a certain amount, of calories. The goal was to get down to a percentage of body fat entitling him to be perfect for the day of competition. To make sure he reached his goal, it was necessary for me to purchase, the exact type of yogurt, meats, and other foods at the grocery store. This became a depressing act of repetition for me. There was a price to pay if I made mistakes. And walked on eggshells. It was my duty to keep the children away from foods in the refrigerator explicitly for his success; otherwise, he became angry and relentless I should follow the rules.

Matt had a way to make you feel bad about yourself if you did not comply with his needs. By nature, a self-assured individual, at this juncture he pretty much caused himself, and me unhappiness. And, although, the lifestyle he conjured up stressed our family, I cannot say, and will not say it was all his fault. He was my partner 'for better or worse', and I tried to make him happy at the cost of my personal anxiety. Trying to comply with all the rules for his success fear and sadness crept on me like a heavy veil, and it was dragging me down. My entire life had been filled with fear causing me grief. I was not about to live in another environment where chaos was brought on by another controlling character. What had I done? Why did I take this route? I thought I finally found semblance in my new world. However, it was not so. I had learned early on, "a leopard does not change its spots". I had not changed mine. Why would anyone else?

We often fought about his idiosyncrasies. But being Amy, I stuck in there. After all, I thought to myself, "it's ok," he will revert back to his old self when the competitions were over. Actually, it was difficult not to admire his diligence and dedication to stick to a strict diet and daily work out. Matt's body had been transformed into a muscular, competitive physique. No fat cells deformed his body. As a family, we attended all the competitions to support Matt.

On stage, he became our hero, and we were entirely convinced he would be able to compete at a professional level. To ensure success one must place first in your weight class at the competition. This was a challenging goal. He managed 5th place, but was not disappointed, and was determined to carry on in order to receive a Pro Card. It is the golden ticket and proves you have dedicated yourself to the work and competed in amateur level bodybuilding competitions and won. At one point, his efforts were honored with a full photo of his physique profiled in a competition magazine. Yes, I was in a constant state of utter aggravation with Matt; however, we were all proud of his prominence in the sport.

He continued his efforts to triumph. I was honestly happy for his perseverance. But after each trophy he acquired, my heart was saying, I hope this is the last. Each time he readied for competition, he turned into a bear. His ambition began to take a more serious toll on our relationship.

I felt such emptiness. For me, each day became a struggle to find solace. Once again, depression and anxiety became my constant companions. While the years crept on, my need to pray more fervently for peace and security dominated my spirit.

As a result of Matt's addiction to his bodybuilding and demands on me, I began to take trips to stores and malls to purchase unessential merchandise. Convinced these material objects would satisfy my yearning for happiness, love and peace was an ongoing obsession. As my anxiety peaked, I became a shopaholic. The items in the shopping bags did not satisfy my fractured heart; and I lived in total denial of the destructive habit I had included as part of my daily life. I don't think Matt was ever aware when I carried into the house bags filled with items of no real importance. Eventually, I became sullen. But again, we were on our next adventure. Our marriage had huge problems. However, soldiers move on, right?

Here was another opportunity to fill the hole. I was all for it. The thought of change or a new endeavor is an incredible mental distraction when in an already confused state. We needed to make the house a little bigger for our family to function correctly. I would have a new focus and fill the void. However, without contemplating our financial constraints, we moved on to an even bigger folly.

To 'turn the tide', rather than renovating our existing dwelling, we received several quotes from contractors to construct a new home. The new residence would be magnificent. For a while, this was an exciting project and I was up to designing and decorating our new palace. It was a great diversion to watch the foundation being dug and walls being constructed. Looking back, it was the worst decision we ever made. The more options we added to the house, the higher the price became. We ended up securing a five-hundred-thousand-dollar mortgage. Yes, the house was huge and beautiful, but our finances were depleted, and we were in denial. There was no escaping the financial hole we had created.

By all measures I had a good husband, exempting the bodybuilding, and some other characteristics, unfavorable to me within his personality. I resolved my personal feelings and dilemma to the fact 'no marriage is perfect.' Most couples have issues. Do they not? I had the most incredible children; however, the love, happiness and peace, I, at one time thought present with Matt, had become derailed and were now lost to me.

Money-wise, we were in a harmful situation. Living in our palace was terrific until the bills came in. During this time in my life, I determined we were so economically upside down, we needed to do something drastic. At least, I needed to do something drastic. Strangely, I loved Matt, but was not in love with him. I knew this fact and had to face it no matter the end results. Material things did not take the place of despair. Except for the love of my children, nothing else mattered. I seriously began to dislike my husband.

When I was a child, I promised myself I would never allow unhappiness to define my life as my mother had. But here I was, again amid sadness. I wanted to feel love and be in love with a person every day. I was not. Our financial situation became more of a disaster when Matt was laid off from Pfizer. The stress between us became insurmountable. Mentally I was in an abyss and did not believe there was positive emotional ladder in my brain, to help me climb out of the darkness and into the light. To reach the top out of the gloom would take enormous effort however, the hole we had dug together was deep. I now recognized the decisions Matt and I made were severe failures. And, these mistakes had accumulated into unfortunate circumstances. For me, there was only one logical measure for a solution to our problems. A divorce!

It had nothing to do with Matt losing his job. We had been sailing along without any successful navigational business tools. In the beginning, we did not create long-term plans for financial success. However, our marriage had also been unstable for a few years. Matt's job loss had merely been the wave rocking the boat. I had visions of the children and me poverty-stricken. Would we all end up in a tent in the woods like my mother? Would we need to go on Welfare? Would we spend hours at the food bank? My mind was racing illogically. I was battling many demons.

If there was one solid fact I could count on, it was my former career. Although, it was difficult to pick up the creative edge I held previously, I was determined to become independent and sail on my own. I had not practiced my craft in a few years. Indeed, I knew I was a quick learner, and although my plan was scary, it was all I had. I began to figure a way out of the abyss. We had worn each other out and both needed to go in different directions. I was done with the relationship and would rely on myself. Hopefully, I was being watched from above. Hopefully!

In between all this mayhem, we received a call from Harley's wife, Sabrina, soon to be ex-wife. I was at home with Matt, Ceaira, and Jesse when the phone rang. At the beginning of the conversation, she conveyed to me in the past few years Harley had acquired a significant drinking problem. I was terribly sad, as well as surprised to hear this news. The marriage to Sabrina had been going downhill, and Harley had filed for divorce. Apparently, after they separated, his health slowly declined, and he refused to take the prescription medications to protect his heart. The diagnosis was poor. I also learned Harley had become depressed and believed he had no hope for a long life. His mental and physical health spiraled downward. Apparently, the drinking became even more of a problem as the years had gone by. I was happy Ceaira was with me in Connecticut during the times of Harley's decline. She had not been aware of the severity of her dad's condition.

However, this was not the worst news I learned from Sabrina. Harley had bought a motorcycle and one night decided to go on a drinking binge while with his new girlfriend. He then left the woman at the bar and was riding at a tremendous speed when spotted by an undercover police officer in an unmarked car. The officer turned on the flashing light he had placed on the roof and initiated the siren. The chase was on. Harley had refused to slow down and stop. He tried to outrun the officer, lost control of the bike and crashed into a tree only yards from his home. Actually, unconsciously, he had simulated the same type of vehicular accident as his mom had, just around the corner from his home. The alcohol and his negligence caused a horrible tragedy. Badly hurt, the ambulance was called to take him to the hospital, where it was learned he had sustained significant injuries to the chest. Harley was conscious when he was admitted to the emergency room.

After the call, Ceaira and I immediately traveled to Virginia. Throughout the trip, we both fervently prayed for his considerable recovery. She could be with her dad through this awful time. When we arrived, Harley was still conscious. Ceaira was able to converse with her father a little. It was so sad to see this still young man in such a wretched condition. We were able to see where Harley was swollen and bruised on his face and his arms. Ceaira held her daddy's hands, and he told her he loved her and would soon be home. It was not meant to be. This was the last time Ceaira would see her dad alive. Shortly after they talked, he went into a coma and was placed on a respirator. His already fragile heart could not deal with his ravaged body. It was so odd his mom, Denise, died the same way, crashing a vehicle so close to her house, just a few steps from her front door.

Family and friends had congregated at the hospital and tensions were high. The Peyton family was convinced Harley will pull through. He was still legally married to Sabrina. The divorce had not been finalized. Sabrina and the family began to argue. She was still legally his wife and had the right to turn off the respirator. She wanted to unplug him and was bound and determined to have all the life- saving equipment removed. The family was horrified; nonetheless, it was Sabrina's legal decision. I am sure she knew Harley would be in a terrible state if he had survived the trauma all broken up, and unable to live a normal life. Also, sadly, his brain cells were not showing any chance of recovery. On June 8, 2007, the country boy left the mountains, rivers, streams, woods, and fields he so loved to enter into the Hands of God.

When Ceaira and I returned home to Connecticut, I buttoned up my thoughts of unhappiness with the marriage and tried to keep the family together for a little longer. Ceaira was grieving for Harley, and in a way so was I. We had had a history together. However, the financial drain between Matt and me hovered over us while we continued to occupy the palace. It had become terrible burden. Luckily, within a short time, we sold our home. For the present this seemed to fix our revenue problems, but it did nothing to solve my persistent feelings of emotional discontent. However, again we made another mistake and together rented a house. Why I agreed to this move is truly beyond my comprehension. At the time, and as usual, my judgment was senseless. I was hanging on knowing full well I had made the wrong choice.

Chapter Twenty-Three
Matts in My Rearview Mirror

THE RELATIONSHIP HAD LONG AGO lost any love or passion it may have had, and I did not see myself as a permanent companion to Matt. Finally, after eight years, courage, along with a great deal of anxiety, as well as the ever-increasing emptiness in my soul, took over and I told him I wanted a divorce. Ceaira played a role in my decision to leave Matt. She knew me well and, time and again, she would say to me she thought I was not happy. Although she loved Matt, she wanted what was best for me.

I gave Matt many reasons why I wanted a divorce and, specifically, was sharing with him the fact I had a massive void in my soul I was not able to fill. His bodybuilding became my nemesis. I was tired of the endless arguments ensued between us and did not want our son, Jesse, exposed to our issues. Matt was totally shocked and felt I was giving up on him, and he did and said everything in his power to change my mind. But again, I was stalwart in my decision. I wanted out. And, I left asking for no alimony or child support. For some strange reason, I had no fear of my financial future. I felt sorry for Matt, but he deserved to be with someone who could tolerate his strong feelings to achieve his goals and love him at the same time. Deep down he probably knew this was a good move for both of us.

Chapter Twenty-Four
My Best Friend Cassie

ASSIE WAS A FRIEND OF both Matt and me. I met her through a real estate agent who handled the listing for our home. We instantly became close and chummed around with each other through my marriage with Matt and became closer as my marriage spiraled downward. We both were going through a divorce at the same time and together were dealing with all the financial and emotional trials presented to us. Two gals who married too young, we never managed to sufficiently experience the single life.

Through a friend, I found a small apartment for rent I could afford. When I first visited the place, the man who owned it said to me, "Someone helped me once when I needed it. I want to help you so I will rent it to you reasonably." I was so grateful. It was mine. It had only one bedroom, but Ceaira had moved in with her boyfriend, Hanna now had her own place. I would convert the living room into a bedroom for Jesse.

The half-million-dollar house was a memory; however, my soul soared with delight in the coziness of this little one-bedroom sanctuary. During this time, there was no other family around me except Ceaira and Jesse. My darling Hanna, Aunt Angie's daughter, had moved away. Cassie's family had now become my family. I was always invited to her family home on holidays. She has been with me through great times and terrible circumstances, I cherished her friendship. When I finally told her Matt, and I had broken up, she came to my apartment in her pajamas and sat with me while I cried my eyes out, and suggested we go for a long ride to talk out my emotional crisis.

She actually believed our breakup was temporary and we both needed time to sort out our feelings. Although, I was delighted with my new place and life, there were many times after the split I became melancholy. Perhaps the casualties of my past life had snow-balled and released itself when I was unequivocally free. Many instances when I faltered, Cassie would come to the apartment and get me out of bed, make me dress. We ventured off to find a new distraction to turn my newfound depression around. For me, this new independence was a huge step, and sometimes as brave as I thought I had become, the ultimate escape at moments became daunting.

Cassie adored Ceaira, whose silly and witty personality kept her laughing continuously. No one could find a more caring and sympathetic friend. I consider this dear person another of God's angels, sent to help and save me from moments of great anguish. One's life, at a crossroads, is a place in a mind where a moment's split-second decision catapults, one into the unknown. The road chosen may be successful or unpromising; presently unknown future plans may be jeopardized without careful thought and vigilance to a specific problem large or small. And, God knows, I had created enough mistakes in my lifetime to last forever. After leaving Matt and finally adjusting to my new life as a part-time single parent, eventually, my lifestyle began to change. I now had great fun finding new places to hang out, have drinks, dance and meet all types of new friends. Yes, I was happier. Finally, free, my confidence level soared.

Matt and I did not have an ugly divorce. Together, we worked out all the details. Jesse's well-being was our priority and Matt rose to the occasion. We would split our time so both of us would take responsibility for our son. And worked as a team for the benefit of the child we adored. Since I never asked for child support, we financially, equally, divided whatever Jesse required. Remaining friends throughout the divorce to this day has been the best evidence for our son's emotional security. Actually, we are better at being friends than as a married couple. Our personalities are so different. Priorities collided too many times. I don't believe we were ever meant to be together forever. However, we do share this fantastic son. I admitted to myself I am an eccentric, free-spirited person; whereas,

Matt is extremely structured, self-determined and severely self-directed. We share equal time with Jesse. We co-parent extremely well. Our son enjoys and has different world views, due to the polar opposite personalities of his parents. This works exceptionally well for Jesse.

Cassie and I both married young and had never really experienced the single life. It was a joy to have someone as a friend who wanted to explore the new world lifestyle we created. Taking advantage of any free evening to bar hop, dance, and make new friends was so different for me. I relished the idea of just being able to do what I wanted without interference from others.

In the interim, Matt's life seemed to unfold very well. He had reconnected with a girl named Barb who had worked with him at Steak Loft when we first arrived from Virginia. Although they had no relationship at the time, they coupled romantically after Matt and I divorced. She had three boys from a previous marriage. In age, Jesse fits between all three kids. It didn't take long before Matt and Barb married and had a baby together. They brought another boy into their life. I actually adore Barb. She is a perfect stepmom for Jesse.

Unbelievably, we all get along wonderfully and share a lot of activities as a family, including vacations and Jesse's football games. Matt and Barb are very much in love and make a perfect couple. He really is a good guy and deserves happiness. It just didn't work with or for me. Jesse gets along with all his stepbrothers and adores his baby brother. He loves residing at his dads with all the commotion, and yet is thrilled when returning to my home where life is quiet. This part of the arrangement could not have worked out better

Book Eleven

Chapter Twenty-Five
Marco, Love, Finally?

"and she loved a boy, very much.
even more than she loved herself."

~Shel Silverstein, Author,
The Giving Tree

MARCO AND I WERE ACTUALLY introduced at a friend's birthday party in May of 2009. The event took place in the dance club at Foxwoods Casino, Stonington, Connecticut. Years before the event, and on occasion, I remember seeing him at different venues; sometimes at Mohegan Casino also in Connecticut. I was enamored with his striking looks and what appeared to be a relaxed manner. To me he looked extraordinarily handsome, and magnetic. This particular night I had been divorced for over a year. Truthfully, I had no intention of having an affair. I sincerely believed, after an eight-year marriage, and previous failed relationships I had had enough anxiety trying to be content with my male partners. My emotions were in check. This was the very first time in my life I was actually alone. Jesse was with his dad more often than not, and I was managing very nicely on my own. I did not want or need any complications to spoil my carefree, and joyful lifestyle. I loved socializing with new friends and living life spontaneously. This entire existence I had created for myself was wonderfully freeing. In truth, the first time Marco was in my sights, I was still married to Matt. Although our relationship was strained, we were continually acting the role. Interestingly, Matt was with me on a few occasions when Marco had been present at many of the venues. I looked but did not touch.

The past year as a single person had been divine. Freedom is a marvelous, self-gratifying, experience. It had also been the very first time in my life I was not bound to another individual, including a roommate, who could possibly interfere in my precious independence. I became aptly surprised at how well I functioned. Due to my ability to now focus on personal success, I became exceptionally creative in my career as a make-up artist and hairstylist; and pleased when I accomplished a specific, if not challenging, hairstyle desired by a client. And, of course, the money I earned was now specifically to spend on Jesse and me.

This was not how my voyage through life began. I was always committed to another person, my mother, Harley, Matt. I loved to dance, so I spent a lot of time in places where I was able to let loose and be happy. Life became joyful. I began to feel full of hope and, finally, at peace.

The unforgettable night we were introduced, I suddenly became conscious of an instant connect with Marco. This man, so stylish and impeccably dressed, an Adonis with a conservatism about him had a magnetic sensual aura. For the first time I understood the unexpected, aroused emotions within me I never knew existed. Resisting these provocative feelings had tested my sensual desires like no other. The man next to me had captured my pleasure seeking spirit. I could not escape the passionate, innate urges dominating my entire body. Telling myself I was being ridiculous, I simply laughed at myself regarding the possibility of this potential, risky relationship. However, this was the passion I have always been hoping for. He was irresistible. Emotions were reeling, and I almost believed I knew him from somewhere far in the past. Of course, I never met him before. We talked and danced, and, when we danced close, we melted into one another's skin. When it was time to leave all my friends walked to their cars separately, except Marco and me. While standing alone together, we had a short conversation, then I found myself exchanging telephone numbers. My head was spinning as thought I were a *junior in high-school*. I was enamored and wanted to devour him whole. This first encounter with Marco was the beginning of a beautiful friendship and for better or worse, passionate, and, possibly complicated affair; and, of course, the sexual attraction was tremendous. Yes, I had let my guard down.

In the beginning, I was very much enjoying his friendship. He did not come around much and because of the age difference, I never imagined the relationship would become too dangerous. Marco was fifteen years my junior. I envisioned us as friends. Friends were always lovely to be around. As time wore on, we managed to be closer, and one evening, we became too passionate, eventually leading to sex.

After all, sex was good with friends. No serious talk, just lovely, pleasing, sex! In spite of my commitment to freedom, I felt comfortable with Marco. My brain was telling me I was just infatuated with and, sorely, attracted to this mild-mannered and charismatic man. However, intimacy was not easy to turn down. It had been well over a year since I had had sex. I am sure my body was starving for this all to natural experience.

In the following weeks I looked forward to Marco's telephone calls each evening. Although born in Albania, his family emigrated to Italy, then immigrated to the United States from Italy. His heavy Italian accent was not always easy to interpret. Understanding him became a challenge and, apparently, I wanted to take it on. I was delighted with myself if I understood fifty percent of what he was saying. Most often, due to his lack of speaking reasonably well at times and not following some of the English language basics, I began to help him with his personal business issues. We worked together so I could teach him to pay his bills. I would write his checks for him and went as far as helping him purchase a vehicle. He also learned to cook breakfast for himself with a little help from me.

However, I believe, the most critical task was in helping him "learn how to love and have fun." This is in my nature. I loved sharing adventures. He had said he could not love. Trying to survive as an immigrant was a difficult task for him. Evidently, he found it arduous to entertain himself with any fun ideas and desires. His work ethic always interfered with his ability to balance pleasure with work. What he did enjoy was going to the casino with his brothers. I remember taking him bowling for the first time in his life. He was so non-flexible. And, he made me laugh with his bewildered smile. The ball was such a foreign object to him. He merely stared at it most of the time. I really do not think he enjoyed this particular sport. I wanted to show him so much more, but he did not have time. He had never been to a Zoo or an amusement park. We really loved each other's company.

I introduced Marco to many people and tried to have him feel like he fit in. Actually, I believe when I first met Marco, I was his only real friend; also, I emphasized there was much more in life than work and money. Eventually, he did seem to aspire to many pleasures. At times, he shared with me, how I indeed showed him love and how to love. He said his heart opened.

Marco always stated he loved being with me; unfortunately, not enough to tell his family he wanted to be with me permanently. I surely enjoyed sharing new aspects of my world with him. It was like opening the eyes of a little kid to new adventures. As the summer came upon us, we began to see each other quite often. When my son Jesse was at his dad's, Marco would find his way to my place after work and spend the night. Then we began enjoying the company of both our friends; however, our relationship was non committable on his part. He was a diligent worker spending many hours at a construction site, where the family owned and operated business; and, our time together became limited. He always made an extra effort to join the crowd on weekends, however, many times I was lonely for him during the weekdays. The work ethic was inspired by loyalty to his immediate ethnic family and their businesses, loyalty to one another, and the familiar people within the same culture. Although, Marco was brought up in Italy and spoke Italian, his roots were in the Caucasus an area between the Black and Caspian Seas in the Region of Eurasia. The people in these zones were strong minded, and severely work oriented.

As time went on, I suggested for once we go out to dinner alone without friends, in a quiet atmosphere. It was, actually, our first real date. Up until this moment all of our socializing had, mostly, included a large crowd. When he agreed, I could not believe I had butterflies in my stomach and was actually acting like a teenager. We learned a great deal about each other on the first real date. The most important fact he related to me was our age difference caused him some anguish. Marco always acted so maturely. Recognizing the difference, I visualized a downward spiral in the relationship. This affair could cause chaos for his family, and my children.

Ultimately, for me to explain the fifteen- year age gap to Ceaira would be a nightmare. I was at a defining moment regarding this problem.

More than not, the feeling of love suppressed the negative aspects of this seemingly madcap relationship. Yes, the sparks were flying, actually way too much! I knew I was looking for trouble. Could I stop? God help me!

Caring so profoundly for this sweet and mild-mannered man, I most often ignored the age discrepancy. Marco and I were having too good of a time. He was gentle, kind and loyal. I fooled myself into thinking I wasn't looking for a long-term relationship, and just loved being with this fantastic person; and for the first time, I didn't believe I loved the idea of love. I thought I had developed a friendship and romance with a remarkable person.

The rules of life and society have a way of turning feelings upside down; and when allowed logic and reality could be staunch, unshakable companions. If I were honest with myself, I would learn this as time passed, and the pain would be indescribable. He was so attractive, attentive, and pure of heart, it had become difficult to go back and resume a platonic friendship. I should have realized we crossed the line after our first sexual encounter.

As summer progressed, my lover began to spend more time with me overnight. Never had I felt this passionate sexual attraction with any other man. With a young son still at my side, guilt had begun to interfere with my emotions. I did not want Jesse to believe Marco and I were any more than friends, so I made sure he was not around him much.

However, there was a more significant issue. I had an eighteen-year-old daughter. Although she wasn't living with me, she was around the house quite a bit, and had not been fooled, nor was she happy with a man not much older than her. Young children may overlook certain aspects of a relationship. Teenagers don't miss a beat. The water was rising, and I was drowning in a sea of complex problems.

One morning, Ceaira stopped by while Marco and I were having breakfast. My teenage daughter never believed she needed to hold back her opinions when she did not like a situation involving me. As usual, the thoughts in her brain had a direct route to her mouth. Stoically looking at Marco, she said, "What are you doing with my mother?" He replied nervously in his Italian accent, making him seem vulnerable and ill-confident, "I don't know. We are good friends." She then stated, "Well, I can tell you this right now, she is too old to have any more children to take care of, and even if she thinks about getting married again, I will kill her!" She was bold and probably had more sense than me. At the same instant of her diatribe with her caustic comments, my daughter embarrassed, fractured, and somewhat made clear to me the confused thoughts in the recesses of my own brain. I asked her to stop chastising him. Marco was squirming in his seat, as though he had been berated by a grade-school teacher. Ceaira continued her tirade by informing Marco, and me, "I deserved better," and he was "too young for me." Finally, I could not control my wounded emotions and yelled at her to stop, then stole for the bathroom where I just cried and cried. It appeared I was the child and Ceaira the adult. What a disaster!

A few days after the incident Ceaira's words frequently resonated in my thoughts and allowed me to really think about my relationship with this young, and loving man. The random, emotional crying jag finally abated, and I, again, realized Ceaira, as usual, knew me very well. In truth, I had in my head, secretly fallen in love with Marco. Although it was wrong for her to lash out at him, she had made a stand for my benefit. The entire incident was a turning point in our relationship. What could our future become with this vast age difference?

Ironically, a few days before I had received a call from my Cousin Susan, she stated to me this entire relationship with Marco was based on just having some summer fun, great sex, and I would be done with him come Fall. About the same time, other friends began to express opinions about Marco and me. A few envisioned the relationship flourishing. Apparently, these friends were more liberal. Others believed our relationship doomed. I believe these friends were probably more realistic. If I was thinking realistically, perhaps this was the time to accept the inevitable. Our relationship was on a steep slope, and it was heading for disaster.

Although, the relationship seemed destined to an unfortunate end, it was Marco who truly had given me something I never experienced before, a full heart. At times, I even imagined having a baby with him. I knew his calm and gentleness. A great father, I am sure.

Book Twelve

Chapter Twenty-Six
Ceaira Breaks

ALSO, CONFRONTING ME AT THIS time came a more serious problem. As Ceaira entered her late teens, her heart condition became worse. She began to have mini blackouts. During a visit while at a friend's home, she fell down a flight of stairs during a blackout. We knew it was time to implant a defibrillator in her chest. Her fears for her own future were surmounting. Not only was she physically impaired, but she also began having panic attacks. Her dad had had a defibrillator implanted. However, due to his procrastination to visit The National Institute of Health in Maryland, as well as his denial of the disease, Harley averted the necessity to keep up with defibrillator maintenance. And, without his doctor's supervision and medical orders, he may have helped cause his final demise.

Since the disease was congenital and she knew many of the family members had succumbed, Ceaira was filled with fear. The only medication she was taking during this time was a blood thinner. Then the doctor prescribed Xanax. She liked the drug. It helped with her anxiety, and she began to treat herself to more frequent and sizeable doses. Ceaira was more than fragile. In prayer, I pleaded with God to help my daughter.

With a sense of urgency, I set up a date to have the device inserted. One concern, and evident for a young girl, was the shape and protrusion of the mechanism visible on her chest by others. Usually, this instrument is placed in older individuals who sometimes have more meat on their body to hide the obtrusive life-saving instrument. Ceaira was so young and thin, if she was wearing a bathing suit, one would see the box on her chest. A significant worry for a young girl's self-esteem.

The positive side of this dilemma was Ceaira began to visit a physician she really liked. The suffering child had visited so many doctors in her life. It always became agonizing when she knew it was time again. The new cardiac physician explained the procedure in terms we could both understand, and my child finally began to have hope and feel more comfortable with the insertion of the new device. The heart surgeon with whom we now had complete faith mentioned with the help of a plastic surgeon, the defibrillator would be placed under her left breast. This procedure would allow the breasts to remain the same size. It was this physicians' first experience to try a new technique; however, he appeared extremely confident.

Ceaira was in surgery for almost five hours. I was a critical mess. With forced patients, and again relying on my faithful friend, God, I prayed continuously throughout the crucial hours for her to be safe and alive. Finally, after all the time under anesthesia and in the operating room, unconscious, separated from me behind surgery doors, and during a time of parental desperation; I had finally been notified the procedure had been successful. Phew!

After a few days in the hospital, she recovered sufficiently to be discharged, and decided to temporarily come and live with me. Pain pills were prescribed, and Ceaira managed nicely while laying around the house recuperating for a few weeks. My child was feeling so confident, both her breasts were the same size, and she was now safe from any major blackout catastrophes.

After playing a game with her friends by lifting her shirt up and down many times to show off where her new unseen mechanical lifesaver could not be viewed, she joked about being the bionic woman. I was confident we had reached a milestone. She also joked about the surgery, as if it was just a little hiccup. However, the joy did not last.

When Ceaira took the pain pills, she became a different person, moody and belligerent. At first, I dismissed the behavior and thought it reasonable after all she had been through; and, I waited for her to resolve her spirits. Many times, while visiting different doctors, she complained of pain. Each physician knowing her serious health issues prescribed more

Xanax for anxiety; and, finally, Oxycodone for pain. Coupled with her many physical and mental problems, Ceaira was unable to sleep and was then prescribed Ambien. I then realized she knew how to manipulate doctors to give her exactly what she wanted. The problems brought on by her extended period of taking heart medications after each heart surgery, had worn on her and she had struggled with addiction and depression since she was nineteen years old.

At the time of her recent crisis, I had inconveniently been dealing with my own struggles regarding her physical condition. Although the surgery went well, I anticipated all sorts of problems to come. Not equipped to handle Ceaira's addictions, I lacked the necessary tools to help her cope. Knowing I had given her the best childhood, I wanted her to have everything I did not have. I believed throughout her life she had received all the love a mother could provide. I hugged her often and regularly. Every day I announced my love for her. She had everything material a child could wish. However, she was a child in a physical and mental crisis.

When Ceaira began to use drugs regularly, I felt enormous guilt and chided myself and was sure I had failed as a parent, but how and why? Although knowing I never left her out of any decisions reached by me, I blamed myself for all the past failed relationships I had had in the past. I know Ceaira wanted me to be happy, but I also believed it was hard on her when I divorced my second husband, her stepfather, Matt. Compiled with the loss of her dad and dealing with a life-threatening heart condition living life became unbearable for my sweet girl.

Then suddenly, for a brief moment, our lives again turned positive when Ceaira surprised me and enrolled in a nursing program at a community college. Actually, her grades were better in college than in high school. My daughter became passionate about a future career in nursing. She had been in and out of doctor's offices and hospitals all her life. My lovely girl was adamant about becoming the kindest caring professional possible.

Unfortunately, in no time with the continued use of many medications for her heart, pain, and coping daily with anxiety, she began to miss classes. Her claim was "school was stressing her out." She did an excellent job of hiding how much medication she was taking at one time, and her character had transformed itself into an entirely different individual.

Looking into her eyes became scary. It broke my heart to see my daughter in this way. Now she began to sleep most of the time and through many of her classes. When I initiated conversations regarding problems I foresaw, with the many opioids consumed, she denied everything and left the house. Eventually, she became tired of my interrogating, and requests for her to receive help and she moved out. Ceaira moved in with her boyfriend, Randy, and his family. He was a sincere and honest person and loved her. Eventually, her addiction became more evident, and he was devastated with her desire to continually state she needed medication for her pain. This caused friction in their relationship. He told her if she did not get help, he would break up with her. After many requests from Randy, and with his help, Ceaira was admitted to a treatment center in Rhode Island. She was in the Rehab center for a few weeks and managed to write the most distressing words in her journal while there.

10/19

Today is my first night here and my mom just left, I feel really scared, and like I shouldn't be here.

I know my Depression is Bad but I always thought I would just get threw it. my depression was down and under control for awhile. until school and work became unsteady I finally Hit bottom really hard. I am here now and I can't get Randy off my mind. I hope I can show him the better part of me. I also hope my mom will see how much I Love her and appretieadet everything she does for me.

I had a very good childhood. Very spoiled I know see all the great stuff I had and people who loved me. One thing that lead me up to this was my Dads Death He never got to know how much I Love him and how much I did care.. That was hard. Also the Divoirce of my mom and Matt at first I thought it would not bother me as long as my mother was happy. However it did hurt I feel so Bad for everything I put Matt threw when I really did care! I should be thankful and This is another thing that makes me very upset.

I Love my mom but I feel like she could be doing better for herself and that hurts.I also feel as if I let her Down and thats the last the last thing I want. Another thing is living with my BF Randy. I Love him very much and want to be with him alot but I know I can't. living with his family is good because They care so much, it is Bad Cuz they r not my family. They can be a hard living situation and I need to be on my own to get a better mindset and be mor Independent !

Ceaira

10/20

What I would like to do is try to show the people I love that I apreshaite everything they have Done for me . This is MY MOM Randy ! MATT Randy's MOM. I want to set a plan for my self to get on my own two feet ! I think it will be best to stay with my mom and Save money for my own place.I need a good job to keep myself happy. I have a new ataitude towards's life, and that's to enjoy it. I feel very Bad for putting all this stress on Randy that's not right, hurting him makes me very upset.

Ceaira

I now had two people to consider. Relieved Ceaira was in safe hands, it allowed me to believe there was hope for a healthy rehabilitation. I was also sure Jesse's venturing to his father's home on evenings and weekends would be an ideal situation for him to be away from the unpleasantness surrounding us.

Needing a mental break, I appeased my own personal heartbreak without concern for the consequences. Embarking on a marathon of bar hopping with friends on Friday nights I began drinking and continued even through some Sundays. When I was out with friends, it was less painful for me to accept all the negative issues in my life.

My daughter had been journeying on the wrong path, and this alone gave me intense mental pain. Everything I aspired to stay away from my entire life seemed to be planted on her. I did not smoke and had worried about my mom's health my whole life. She consistently had a cigarette in her hand or between her lips. Ironically, since Lenny smoked, he did not defer from buying cigarettes for her, although he skimped on other necessities.

As a child, I would hide cigarettes in strange places, so my mother could not find them and be tempted, and always hoped she would quit this addiction. I remember when my childhood friends tried cigarettes and asked me if I would like to join, I declined. I did not want to put anything unsuitable in my body. Ceaira smoked. And, racked with sadness I now sought alcohol as a diversion. Obvious, and undeniably so, to say Ceaira and I were both wreaking havoc on each other was a perfect declaration.

Early on I had seen what drugs, alcohol, and cigarettes did to my family and I knew I was going to be different. Never a drinker in my youth; it all changed when I was twenty-one years old. Now and then I would have a beer or two when socializing. When I married Harley, it was normal for girls of the hollows to drink beer. I merely followed the social mores of the community during our marriage. But it was minimal to say the least. When I divorced him, there was no longer a desire or need. For most of my young life, I was resilient to addictions and knew how easy it was to take a fateful road to destruction; and it terrified my tender soul. Unfortunately, I neglected to think about this outcome, as my life with Ceaira and other relationships spiraled downward. I knew I was not an alcoholic, however, in later years after Ceaira's decline and the ongoing futile relationship with Marco, I managed to go against the standards I had long ago enforced for myself.

My pain was often intolerable. I was definitely not aiming to proclaim myself a responsible parent. To relieve the guilty feelings now dominating my emotions I assured myself I was entitled to certain pleasures. I had not attended college and never benefited from the let-loose years many of my age had enjoyed. I fooled myself believing this was my time. All systems were in denial. Yes! I had some fun times, but I regret my night trips to soften my damaged soul more often than not.

Although, I had a few praiseworthy relatives and friends who supported me during my chaotic life, I seemed to have many misconceptions regarding how to handle difficult circumstances. I had turned to God for help during past times; however, all too often, I associated my life with riding on a roller coaster at an amusement park and not enjoying the thrilling ride, indeed not in a sense it is meant to be. The ups and downs of life were daunting at best. It appeared I had often tried to correct my life path, but my personal experiences had sometimes led me on a notorious, self-destructive ride; and during the bad times, I seemed to spiral down on the rails. When I asked God to help, I was not sure he heard me.

As a distraction to all the problems, going out at night with friends helped me to alleviate the agonizing thoughts of Ceaira's multiple medical and addiction issues, as well as Marco's significance to my life and future. I was well aware, Ceaira's health condition could be compromised and it was surely disturbing. Having Marco around made me feel happy and at peace when he was available. However, he was not always within reach.

Unfortunately, I knew I liked him too much. Perhaps I loved him. Actually, my heart was saying I loved him, and I never felt this way towards any in any of my past relationships. I began to think about what we actually had in common. In our separate lives, under different social and economic circumstances, we each suffered hardships growing up. He worked diligently for everything he had in his life. So, did I, however, his family were close and always there for each other and I was alone and on my own. I was not ignorant of the fact his family had struggled with being immigrants; and, fitting in with their present community was a difficult transition for the lineage or pedigree.

Marco's tensions were still in the backdrop regarding family work or relations. I was unable to battle with the loyalty he had to his relatives and community. I was an outcast once again not fitting in. He did not act twenty-four and appeared to have more maturity than most men my age; however, since he laid claim to be the youngest of eight children his wisdom was built on his ability to be independent at an early age. With a family as large as his, sometimes the youngest is a make it, or break it, kid. He needed to grow up fast; his siblings were way ahead of him on life's journey. A massive sense of responsibility and honor always preceded any decisions to divert energy away from the family. I could not now or ever hope to compete with the tribe.

And although a great conversationalist in his ethnic language, our dialogues were a little off due to his vernacular commentary. We often laughed over the difference in interpretations and descriptions of places were sometimes confusing. I loved our strange banter; however, the language barrier could at some point be a problem to our future relationship and family relations. I ascertained when I was with him and his family, I would become an outsider. Frankly, if I were present, I would have been offended if Marco's family commiserated about me in their foreign language. I do not think they ever talked about me in their language, but it was frustrating not knowing what was being said.

My mind was reeling with thoughts of our future together. What would happen in the future? He was twenty-four. I was thirty-nine. He had never had children. Would he want them? I wasn't up for having more babies. By the time our child would be ten, I would be forty-nine. It just did not make sense. He worked for his family in construction and at their restaurant. Would he want to do this job forever? Construction jobs are strenuous and hard on the body. Would he burn out when I most needed him? Would he want to take on another career or schooling? Would it be necessary for me to take on two jobs to support him while he educated himself? Would I look in the mirror five years down the road and think he is in his prime and I am heading into the realm of Senior Citizenry. Would I have to deal with male menopause? Would he become flirtatious when other younger and more attractive women were around? Reality is hard and harsh. There were too many unknowns.

I could not stop thinking about Ceaira and her previous outburst. The particular scene in my apartment was in my thoughts almost daily. She was right and I knew it. Although I had such deep feelings for Marco, his age would always be a concern or problem. If these issues were ever-present in my mind, I was probably now facing the truth. Frightened about the eventuality of our relationship, confusion and fear overwhelmed my senses. I was hopelessly falling in love with this young man; however, my brain, once again, perceived another failing relationship. In spite of these thoughts, I could not dismiss or imagine not having the deep and mild calming effect on me when around him.

Previously in my life, when in a relationship, I never felt such a strong attraction for a man. Now, more than ever I was chained to Marco by these profound and perpetual strong feelings; and did not know how to unleash myself from the grip he had on me. If real love only comes once in a lifetime, perhaps I should grasp the golden ring on the magical merry-go-round I had conjured up myself. Fantasies can be all too realistic in one's mind. I had placed myself in a mindset of uncertainty. Ceaira was ill, and most likely would be for a long time. She needed me. And, Marco was an extraordinary man, who probably would never be in my life as I needed him to be.

Alright! Now I made a decision. I would not have one more failed relationship. This was not going to get any more dangerous. I would not, again, hurt myself by attaching my heart to a connection having too many odds against it and, painfully, began to distance myself from Marco. I still wished to consider him my best friend, and I wanted to be with him so badly it made my heart ache. Don't we usually call on our best friend when we have a problem or need advice? This was going to be torture. I had to stay mentally strong. Would I fail at my commitment to myself to dissolve the affair? I was, again, talking to God. Would he help me?

As I struggled with keeping away from him, he was not making it easy. The plans I made with friends were interrupted by Marco showing up at the same venue and time. I tried not to call him, but he would call me and let the phone ring until I answered. As much as I wanted to distance myself from Marco, he always made an appearance no matter the destination. God, where are you?

This keystone cop comedy went on for a long time. Each unplanned encounter at a gathering or I heard his voice on the phone caused me heartbreak. I suffered separation anxiety; and honestly no longer could cope with the frequent unplanned meetings and marathon phone calls. I was defeated. Reluctantly, I gave in. We were again together, but I somehow felt the need to have negative conversations with him to push him away. I said, "Where is our relationship going from here, Marco?" I told him he needed to leave me and go find someone near his own age. As I spoke these words to him, my heart ached so badly. I felt sad and sick, but I sensed we both knew the truth. He looked at me with tears in his eyes and said, "I will never find anyone like you." I said, "Probably not. I am one-of-a-kind for allowing myself this fantasy to be with you. But who knows, perhaps you will find someone better," and together we laughed. And, I prayed to God to rescue me.

My head told me I needed to let him go so he could date other women and experience the single life. He was young and had never been involved in any serious relationships. I became vigilant in my attempt to push him away. As much as his family appeared to like me, they were more interested in him finding someone his own age and of his culture. My heart was in disharmony.

Once, after a few drinks, I told him he should marry Katrina, a girl approved by his family. Marco looked me in the eye and said, "I don't want to marry her; I want to marry you." I, in turn, said, "That is never going to happen. I will never marry again", and I consistently uttered comments like so to dissolve our fractured relationship. Then, a moment of unexpected truth from Marco, he said, "Why couldn't you just be my age?" I heard the message. It hit a nerve. We now both recognized we were defeated in carrying on this risk filled love affair. A momentous night of reality; we fell asleep so tightly together thinking we could never be pulled apart; however, knowing we had reached "a defining moment." I remember thinking, "I really don't want to lose you." However, the knowledge of Marco's statement surely served to end our love affair. The truth was inescapable. We were now merely going to be friends. At least this fact was what we both recognized. However, our breakup did not end immediately. There were unforeseen, and unbearable circumstances where friendship ruled us to be together. If I were to be honest, deep inside my soul, I did want to be with this man forever. I felt and still do. We had a connection. He is my twin flame.

Apparently, at the time, I was not aware there was a more alarming reason I was not able to break the tie. God knew I would need Marco. One night while sleeping together in bed before our resolution to end the affair, I awakened with a severe headache and paralysis on the entire right side of my body, I could not walk. Marco picked me up and carried me out to the car and drove me to the emergency room. I was so frightened. He was by my side the entire time. Tested by the doctors for any abnormality, I and could see he was terribly concerned regarding my physical, however, most likely, my mental health. The diagnosis was a type of migraine headache and temporary paralysis brought on by stress. I had been so concerned about what was going on with Ceaira at the time, and believed it was the cause of my physical problem.

Although knowing he had his own family to deal with Marco had managed to put everyone aside to help and be with me. His actions to put me first before 'the relatives' through this trauma caused a great deal of stress in his life. The family he belonged to invariably depended on him twenty-four-seven for many of their own complicated issues and business plans regarding their construction company and restaurant. He would work at construction all day and at the restaurant in the evenings. The family was so enmeshed with each other they would do anything for each other whether or not they liked it or had the time. The focus of his relations was only working, earning money and staying tight within the ethnic community. It was his and their life. The mother doted on all of her offspring. All meals were homemade, and she was adamant about baking bread daily. There was no way to infiltrate this close-knit group. Although the generous lot, they kept their distance from outsiders. And there never forgot I was fifteen years older than Marco. This was most definitely a substantial negative aspect of our relationship for the relatives to swallow.

Nevertheless, I was genuinely grateful he was with me during this crisis. My young lover was there for many of the problems I encountered regarding Ceaira during this time. While she had been going through ad-diction, Marco never judged her. He was available to give me advice and support and was sincerely acting like a best friend. After Ceaira was dis-charged from a rehab center, and after her dad's tragic death, she decided to move back to Virginia to stay with her Grandmother Grace. She had had enough of me nagging about her heart condition, taking her meds timely and keeping in contact with her doctor.

I now also believe her leaving was a warning by God; my daughters' choices were going to cause an inevitable outcome. The Lord was getting us ready for us to accept his overpowering future plans for my sweet girl, who was unable to follow a favorable path in life. Her destiny probably could have gone either way. Although she had free fill, somehow, and perhaps, without seeking medical advice with a doctor regarding her heart problem; as well as, without her knowing, or accepting the outcome for abusing drugs Ceaira's choices may have sealed her fate.

After a four-month visit to Virginia, Ceaira called me and announced she had met a guy who she liked a lot and wanted me to meet him. It appeared she had no intention of returning to Connecticut anytime soon, and I really wanted to see her.

By way of our cell phones, we came up with a plan to take a short vacation and meet on the Fourth of July in Myrtle Beach, South Carolina. Marco had agreed to travel with me. There was only one catch, if I could have called it a catch, or a longtime coming. Actually, it was a blessing! Just before we left for our vacation Lenny passed away from cancer. I chose to look at his demise as a blessing from God. The beast was dead. I subconsciously had no intention or desire to honor him by attending his forthcoming funeral. For me, his demise was like releasing a long gush of foul emotional air from my lungs. He was finally leaving the earth; and, hopefully, most of the family who were privy to this loathsome creature would find palliation from his death. I knew my lungs were now clear, however, some deep old blockages may have remained. I thought about going to support my siblings; but since I had plans to see Ceaira and missed her so much; she was my hearts choice. My only thoughts were the excitement felt by me to be with my sweet girl. However, also, during this time I knew nothing about the new boyfriend. Of course, I prayed he would be a good match for her.

When we arrived in Myrtle Beach, I hugged her so tight I never wanted to let her go. She introduced me to her new guy, Connor. Of course, he was a handsome country boy. As we spent time together, he put on a great act, as if he really cared about Ceaira. I did not know what to think about him. But I can tell you, my stomach was roiling with a bad sensation. When I asked Marco what he thought of Connor, he said, "He seems nice, but something about him is not quite right." We were there for only three nights, and Marco and I did not have enough time to know this person. When we said goodbye, my heart sank into despair and I felt I had entered into another abyss. Something was unequivocally strange with this Connor. I sincerely wanted to take her back to Connecticut to sort out this new boyfriend affair and get her to a physician. However, I later learned this was not the plan the Universe intended.

So, imagine the shock when, at nineteen years old, she told me she wanted to move to Virginia permanently. I knew she thought she would have more freedom. After all, I was an ever-doting mother. I also knew she had been affected by drugs after her heart surgery and was probably taking too many opioids. With her addiction problem in tow, she would not have me all over her all the time; and would be alleviated of all the correspondence between her cardiologist, general practitioner and me.

Although she had made this great broadcast to me regarding the new life, she envisioned for herself; in my heart, I believed it would not be long before she would miss me and want to return home. This is how our life together had always been.

Unfortunately, I was wrong. My wish for Ceaira to return to me in Connecticut were not looking good. I learned later this boy she met, Connor, was a problem. There was a rumor in the community he bought and sold drugs. Apparently, she needed the drugs and he would provide her a stash. When I realized her choice of men, I was devastated. I had a sick child with a significant heart condition. Yes, she was nineteen, but in my mind, she was still a child, my child. Prayers were again in the works. Fervent, fervent marathon praying!

At any time, Ceaira could be tossed into a medical dilemma. And without me by her side, she was tempting fate. She had become seriously independent of me and stubbornness kept her from keeping me informed regarding her health.

Marco had been on key. There was definitely a huge problem with Connor. He had a hold on Ceaira regarding her serious drug addiction. Over time, while living in Virginia, Ceaira began acting differently and distancing herself from me. There were long periods without telephone calls. When I did talk to her, she was evasive.

Eventually, she had moved from her Grandma Grace's home in with Connor. I asked my mom, who was living close by, and my brother Danny to check in on her and let me know how she was doing. He told me Connor was indeed selling drugs and believed he was supplying Ceaira. My brother knew Connor and many of the people he hung around with. I was enraged. Sick child! Addicted child! Connor was the worst partner with whom she could have associated. Oh my God, the devil is back, and this time its name is Connor.

The ironic part of the story here is Ceaira was entirely in love with Randy, her boyfriend in Connecticut. He was seriously in love with her and wanted to help her get through her illness and fragile state. Poor guy, at the time, he actually drove to Virginia to try to coax Ceaira to return home. Her life was now in Connors' clutches, and the devil was determined to control her existence. This did not stop Randy from confronting Ceaira about coming back. However, there was a terrible outcome for his journey. When Randy reached the apartment where the two lived Connor pulled a gun on Randy and forced him to leave the apartment. Randy was a big guy, and after knocking the weapon out of Connor's hand, he said some words and, unwilling to take a chance causing a further dilemma left knowing it could all end badly. When Randy returned from Virginia and related the events, I knew I had to travel to Virginia myself and try to encourage Ceaira to come back home. As a mother, I was well aware of her physical broken heart as well as her fragile life. Mothers instinctively appear to recognize when evil forces influence the most devoted and loving children. However, apparently, the need for drugs prevail, always.

Chapter Twenty-Seven
The Desire to Understand

WITH ALL THE SERIOUS COMPLICATIONS regarding Ceaira's health and drug addiction, it was the profound beginning of a strong, strange, and obsessive desire for me to learn more about Jesus. I believed in him. I prayed to him. And, it also was a time when the most incredible, mind-altering events I could have ever anticipated happened before my eyes. My mom told me the few times I attended church with her before I was five years old, I wanted to sit in the front row. She said I was the only little girl who paid attention to the preacher's words, although I did not understand the meaning of the sermon. As a child, I was curious to know who God was and if He was real. I needed to see Him. When I became older, I did not know why God allowed all these bad things to happen to my mom. However, I always prayed to him to help her.

Although I had attended church as a child, I never considered myself a religious person. Yes, I believed in God, and I knew how to pray. As a mother, I did not force religion on my children. However, for some unknown reason, I now wanted to know everything about God, Jesus. I needed answers to my prayers. In the past, I had prayed Lenny would leave my mother and siblings alone. I prayed so hard for something wrong to happen to Lenny so my family would be safe. I knew it was wrong to wish him dead, but we had all been suffering. If there was a devil opposite God, as the preacher said, then our family knew him as Lenny.

When we lived in Medford, I wanted all the fear and suffering to stop. Why would God make all these bad things happen to my family? To say Lenny was one of the disciples of the devil would be cruel and unforgiving. Perhaps as a child, he may have been a mentally tortured soul. As Lenny matured, he may have been influenced by evil forces. If he had been abused in some way, the impulse to torture had a hold on him; and, apparently, the deviant decided to inflict pain on everyone close to him. If his goal was as such, he succeeded magnificently and reached a level of excellence in causing emotional pain, and despair. I often wondered what drove this man. Could he have been one of Satan's disciple's put on earth to cause never-ending havoc? Perhaps some individuals are naturally born with meanness in their DNA. Could it be "The fault of *The Universe?*" One wonders?

When I was a little girl, I had an imaginary friend. I loved *this friend* as a real person. Although I did not know who or what God, Jesus was, something inside of me said, "God is real." I played with my *imaginary friend.* My *friend* was also my protector. At my young age, I believed my imaginary friend was God. I remember loving this *friend* so much, my mother had to have a little talk with me about imaginary friend. She stated, "Imaginary friends are not real." My heart was sick! "But he's my friend, and you believe in God and you can't see him. Why can't my God be real?"

Later, during the times I was able to visit my dad's family, I sometimes attended the Catholic Church. There I learned God was some type of unseen person who people prayed to although he was not a physical being. I began to wonder who God really is. I then began to think if my imaginary friend was not real because no one else could see him what was going on? Who was going to resolve my child's mind dilemma? I really wanted to be able to see the physical God I thought I knew.

Although I had so many conflicting feelings about a real God person through the years, there was something inside of me feeling connected to God, Jesus. This desire to know and confirm perpetuated in my conscious brain all through the years. The need to know who this biblical man, pretty much a stranger to me except for my childhood subconscious memories, became more of an immediate obsession. I then considered my desire to learn a necessity. But I did not know why. This desire or need was something I could not shake off or dispel. I decided the best place to learn about God, Jesus was at the public library. Isn't this the place where people go to learn?

That's me, Amy always needing the facts when I cannot figure something out. If the stories were documented by ancient scholars, perhaps the stories were real. Where else would one get the true story? The story, a legend believed by the faithful was more likely to be the real.

Each time during visits to the library, I checked out as many books allowed. I and rented any and all types of movies, documenting stories about this legendary and mythical person who I was instructed I should have complete faith. As always, I was questing for more answers. I have most often needed tangible proof when confronted with an issue. I wasn't a child anymore, and now as an adult, I could not, in my brain, substantiate my imaginary friend I believed had been real. Or was he?

While I was diligent in my investigation, my brain was in turmoil trying to allow myself to believe in the mystery. I secured a most compelling documentary allowing this confused person to believe in the myth. Through my research, I came across "The Shroud of Turin." I was sincerely fascinated by the marks on Jesus's body caused by the torture he received from the Roman guards. For me, the remnants of sweat and body fluids left by the scourge adhered to the shroud after he was crucified were the proof I needed. I could understand the forms of torture. I could identify with mental and physical anguish, and pain. Here was a moment of total acceptance.

At the beginning of the two weeks while I was investigating "The Truth," I called Ceaira. She told me she had been ill, lacked energy and needed to stay in bed. I was not too concerned. Her illness was most likely the flu. I asked her to give the doctor a call just in case it was her heart. She said, "I'll be okay, after I rest for a couple of days."

Ironically, she also mentioned she had been thinking a lot about God. This was a strange open door. I said, "Ceaira, this is incredible. I have also been thinking about Jesus." She said, "Mom that is so funny! What a coincidence! I am having the same thoughts." We laughed about this familial telepathy. She also mentioned she had been asking her grandmother, my mother Grace, a lot of questions about God, Jesus, and had even requested her boyfriend, Connor, (totally unbelievable he would rise to this request) to read her the Bible every day. With joy in my heart, I told her I had been doing some God searching myself and shared with Ceaira all the material I had been seeking out, as well as the movies about Jesus I had seen. It was a revelation to know Ceaira, and I now had a personal bond that included God, Jesus.

This searching for God was not like the Ceaira, I knew. I believe my child was aware in her subconscious something unfortunate was going to happen to her. Perhaps it was 'her' forewarning from God. At this time, Ceaira did not understand the implications regarding her severe heart condition. Young people sometimes believe they are invulnerable to tragic events. If only she had paid attention to the seriousness of her illness. Perhaps, if she had connected her disease to her need to know about God, Jesus. Probably, God Jesus knew Ceaira was not going to heed the warnings regarding the severity of her illness and was preparing her for her place in "The Lords Realm." Perhaps? Perhaps? Perhaps?

My last telephone conversation with my dearest beloved child was, "I love you Ceaira, get well." She said, "I love you more Mom. Don't worry." And we both disconnected at the same time. I did not know then we had "disconnected" forever.

According to my mother, Grace, who had been communicating with my lovely child; she stated, she had stopped doing drugs and was seriously planning to move back with her grandmother. Mom told me Ceaira was done with Connor and his druggie ways. Mom had always regretted Ceaira did not move in with her before she got sick.

Chapter Twenty-Eight
Encountering a Higher Power

ON MARCH SIXTEENTH, TWO-THOUSAND-ELEVEN, CEAIRA, Rene Peyton would have been Twenty-One-Years old. Before she would have ever reached her birthday, I experienced a journey of unexplainable and incredible events.

One significant Friday evening returning from work, I fell into a strange mood; and, thought I had simply put in too many hours at work. Although usually extremely energetic I became weary. I did not feel ill, just strange. Relaxing on the living room couch for a while to watch a funny comedy I literally could not keep my eyes open to focus. Deciding to turn I immediately fell asleep. Sometime during the night, I awakened to a strange vision catapulting me to sit up straight in the bed. Was I in a sleep/wake state? I will never know the answer. With my eyes wide open there stood the most miraculous entity of God, Jesus one could encounter. Surrounding him were shadowy features of Heaven. There were children running in meadows happily singing. God said, "there was room for everyone in Heaven, and people were simply souls', happy and safe" In my perhaps altered state God said, "no matter what happens, I need to know "He" is everywhere, and angels would always be around me. "Why I was chosen to experience this phenomenon is a mystery? However, the vision came unexpectedly, and it was the first of many mind-boggling strange phenomena. All the extraordinary voices, sights, feelings, and emotions I encountered were as real to me as the sun in the sky, the air we breathe, and the roar of the ocean. During this magnificent time, and adventure, I absolutely, and without a doubt met God, Jesus! Yes, that Jesus, Jesus of Nazareth! Jesus, who died on the cross for our sins. Jesus, who said "He" would return. The King of Kings! And it happened to me, just Amy Lynn, a humble and ordinary human being. I do not say these words lightly because I know, I am to hear negativity and criticism, again, from those who will deny my most extraordinary experiences.

Curious, isn't it? Amy Lynn, a hairstylist who lives in a small community near the shores of the vast Atlantic Ocean. The Atlantic is a powerful organ of the Earth, gigantic and magnificent. Within the seven billion or so humans on earth, I am merely an insignificant entity, not even a head on a pin.

When I awakened on Saturday morning, and after witnessing the images of God, Jesus for an unknown reason I associated the encounter with my imminent death. I was sure it was to be my last day on Earth. God, Jesus did not want me to be afraid I was heading elsewhere into the unknown. However, I had business to take care of; the realities of the new day, work, errands, people to see and meet took over, and I was committed to dot all the I's and cross the T's and finish up before leaving. With human and straightforward thoughts to be in charge, I knew it would be a busy day at work due to the many clients booked, no matter what, where or when, the terrible events I was forewarned of or believed would take place today. I had a responsibility to my job. I could not afford to allow the night's phenomenon to interfere in my day's preplanned agenda.

While driving to my place of work the visual world appeared surreal. The previous night's experience left me preparing myself to say "goodbye" to all the people I cared about and loved. Surely, this was going to be the last day of my life. When it was time to leave the salon, I hugged all my co-workers said goodbye and began to cry. I was so distressed with the grave knowledge of death I was protecting. Surely, this was the end, I left my best and most expensive scissors on the console in my booth for my co-workers to remember me by. I truly believed I would never see them again. I am sure they all wondered if I had lost "one leg of the table." But I was okay with the thought of my demise. This was the direction I was going in due to my interpretation of God's words during the late hours of the evening.

In reality, it was difficult to focus on any of the day's responsibilities. Saturday was always a tremendously busy client day and, as usual, I was obligated to work at a second job. While driving, I was so exhausted, I needed to take a nap before embarking on another shift at my second job. For the last few weeks, I had been waking up frequently during my sleeping hours. Each time the clock read 3:16 AM. I began to assume this would most likely be the time of my death.

Later, I learned and realized the numbers were a significant verse in the Bible, John 3:16, "For God so loved the world that he gave his one and only son, that whoever believes in 'him' shall not perish but have eternal life." It also happened to be the date my daughter was born. I decided to go home and take a short nap, setting the alarm for 3:30 p.m. There would be enough time to get ready for the next shift. When I awakened, the surroundings again appeared surreal. I was exceptionally groggy, and it seemed the physical objects in the apartment were enveloped in a strange fog. I knew I was alive. I was not on psychotropic drugs, but my reasoning ended there. I was surprised when I woke up from my nap and was still here on Earth. I remember saying to myself God, where are you? I am ready.

I forced myself to get ready for the shift. Now, while driving to the destination, I felt as though my body and mind were suspended in time. Visual surroundings were severely fractured. I was sure my soul was getting ready to depart my physical body. God was going to come and take me to "His" home. During this strange personal event, I heard a voice inside my head; just like the voice I had listened to the night before in my encounter or, perhaps whatever state I may have been in. Again, the voice told me, "not to worry, the angels were all around me, and there was nothing to be afraid of."

When I arrived at my second job, one of my co-workers warned me the booked client was downright mean. Usually, I would be dreading this type of person; however, the surreal, slow-witted state I was in afforded me a calmness not even I understood. The lady sat in the chair in my booth with her shoes off and crossed her legs. She did not speak much but provided me with precise details as to how she wanted her hair styled. During the completion of the styling process, while blow-drying her hair,

I looked at her face in the mirror and there were tears streaming down. Again, the God voice I had heard earlier, revealed to me she had cancer.

Later, I repeated the thought to my co-workers. The spa manager overheard me and said, "How could you know this? She does have cancer." Undoubtedly, God was with me for sure.

In the evening of the day I had commented about the woman who had cancer, I continued to hear the voice of God in my head. This one-sided conversation by 'Him' was indeed working against all logic; however, my mind was playing with this surreal state and I managed to let the voice take over. By nature, I am curious and, apparently part of my confused psyche wanted to hear more from this entity. He merely kept talking to me telling me, "Do not be afraid, He would take care of me, and God is Love." It appeared to cement my thoughts of dying. I knew I was on my way out of this physical world. He just did not say when. I determined I had been in a mild, one-sided conversation with God, and I was in preparation for my departure to the unknown. Hopefully, a journey to Heaven.

Actually, many times after the perplexing day, I continued to talk incessantly about God and religion to anyone who would listen to me. As a rule, I would not allow my religious beliefs to become so apparent to my colleagues. Utterly compelled to share what I had learned through my research I continued my obsessive diatribe. It is strange, but I cannot even remember many of the statements I made. But one fact I do remember is, God is Love and "He" lives in all of us. Many of my co-workers, some who were my good friends, began to worry about me.

As the days wore on, I continued my mind's search for the meaning of God, Jesus Christ. Something was gnawing at me. I did not feel right. A dark black cloud was above me, and I could not shake the feeling of doom. I had no inclination it concerned my daughter. I just felt weird. It was also a time of chaos in the world. The doomsayers were preaching God and The Revelation. These souls were confident the world was coming to an end sometime in the month of December 2012. So, I began to think perhaps I was also caught up in the frenzy, and, maybe, a paranoid brain was responding to this apparent preordained world event.

Without hesitation, I journeyed to the bank and removed all my savings. If the financial world was heading for economic devastation should the economy collapse, I would not allow myself to be in a state of financial distress. I stocked my house with food and planned to prepare for the disaster to befall me. It was not happening for almost two years, but I was determined follow the group in their announcement of doom. My friends began to notice my strange behavior. They knew I was agonizing over a future catastrophic event. Little did I know the disaster would be forthcoming; so profound, however, it would annihilate my small world. My life would no longer be what I knew. And indeed, when the tragedy struck, the devastation was irreparable. My Soul was to die, and it would be a long time before it was resurrected.

A month before I lost my daughter, Ceaira, who was twenty at the time, I experienced another journey of unexplainable phenomena. It happened one evening just returning from work. I had been in a strange mood. There is no reasonable explanation of what occurred, confounded, confused, and tilted me beginning February Sixteenth, Two-Thousand-Eleven. I was psychologically and mysteriously catapulted into another level of consciousness. As far as I knew, I hadn't had a mental breakdown and do not believe I was hallucinating. What I do think is, I was extremely fortunate to be entitled to another significant and extraordinary spiritual event.

As the night wore on, I continued to feel I was in some sort of dream state. Why else would I be feeling this way? Furiously, I began to pray. I told God how much I loved my kids and was concerned regarding what would happen to them if I were to die. His voice came to me again. He told me, "go to the window and look up at the streetlight." I obeyed God's voice. When I looked up at the light, there were three reflections. The first was my dear love, Marco. The second was my son, Jesse, but the third reflection kept changing. At first, the face was my daughter, Ceaira, then there were faces I did not recognize. I asked God who the other faces belonged to. "He" said, "it was 'Him' and 'He' was the light. 'He' shines in all the people I love."

Then it began to snow. God told me to look carefully at the snowflakes, each one was different. Imagine, I heard God's voice say, "each one was like the many spirits in heaven." A gentle warm feeling began to permeate my body, and I felt an enormous love I never knew and thought, "how lucky am I to have this conversation with God, Jesus"

Suddenly, there was a knock at the door. I did not want to answer. And, yes, I was afraid. God was coming to take me, but I was not ready to accept this journey. Hesitantly, I proceeded to what I believe would be the *hereafter*. I knew if it was God, the door was not going to stop his entrance. Cautiously, I opened to find Marco standing there. During this moment, a loud gush of wind swept over us. We were both startled by the strange force. There was no explanation. I hugged him tightly not wanting to let go. "Are you alright?" he asked. He said, "from the street, I saw you looking out the window." My brain was paralyzed and could not think or find the words to describe the incredible encounter. He appeared confused. I only just stated to him, I needed some sleep.

We slept together this strange night since I was unable to be alone in my home. But throughout the night the visions became more intense and ephemeral. I believed God was talking to me through the heart and soul of Marco. I wasn't sure if we were awake or asleep. The events were so real to me; I merely accepted "all" the strange illusions happening. Marco would never understand. Of course, I was sure of this fact. What was happening to me?

There was no escape from these fleeting visions. Sleep had now become a challenge. It would not allow me to enjoy its quiet darkness and break free from the alternate surreal world I now lived. My head felt like a plug had been inserted to change the thoughts in my brain and I was a subject of *The Matrix*. Next thing I knew, I heard God's voice like a Clarion saying, "Amy, I am here. I am always with you." But the words were coming through Marco's mouth. However, the unaware person who was next to me in bed was not speaking. The voice was not Marco. It was a different voice. God's! I never believed Marco was God. But I do think he was a vessel through whom God spoke.

We lay in bed face to face as we talked. God and me. This momentous time with "The Savior" was miraculous and unforgettable. Through the conversation, I savored the comfort and love. Marco and I lay in bed with God's voice between us for hours. I had so many questions: I asked God about Heaven. He assured me there was no limit to the joy one would feel with Him in the everlasting. He also mentioned the animals had no fear of being killed and all God's creatures lived together peacefully. We talked about my childhood. He explained to me He had always been there through the most horrific times and also stated, "without knowing the bad, we would never understand the good." Most importantly, the answer to "bad things happen to good people" continues to be a mystery. Events happen to people the way they need to. It is "all" simply part of His plan. We talked about love, and I should not be afraid to love. He was aware of all the problems I had in my life. I did not want the conversation to end and was captured and captivated by the love and spirit of God. The final words God said to me that night was, "Always Trust Me."

Apparently, I fell asleep after this encounter and the next morning, I awakened naturally filled with joy. Obviously, I had not died, but was now in a different zone. It is still unbelievable God came to me in this way. After all, I am only a pebble on the beach of trillions. Of course, I continued to be convinced I was going to die, but I believed it was not ordained at this time. I am now also assured God does speak to us through others to get our attention. Looking back on the events that occurred, I can only rationalize God knew what was going to happen in the weeks following and was preparing me for the final game, and He was going to help me through it.

Assuming Marco was the instrument God used to converse with me I did not mention the incredible night's extraordinary event. Surely, he would think I belonged in the nearest mental institution and would calmly and logically drive me to the nearest facility.

However, not sharing my charismatic meeting with God did not stop me from continuing as an amateur preacher. Occasionally, after I began my conversations with God, Jesus I merely rambled on to anyone who would listen. Never mentioning the extraordinary meeting to anyone, I knew this would be cause for everyone close to me to really be concerned about my mental health. Marco became so troubled with my preaching, he called my best friend at the time, Cassie to talk me out of these strange sermons about God, Jesus. Then, he removed all the books relating to the Divine off the bookshelves and handed the stack of the precious material to Cassie for her to dispose of elsewhere.

The morning after the session with Marco and Cassie, the pair quietly discussed the fact I was most likely suffering from a *spur of the moment* invasive multiple personality disorder. Although, they believed I had gone nuts, I knew no matter what, I had to go to work that day. I called the salon and heard a message for me on the answering machine. The message revealed, "I had no clients scheduled." Strangely, I later learned I did, indeed, have appointments. Free for the day I sat down to rest, and my mind was again on the rat wheel. Obsession now became a constant regarding the incidents during the days and nights of understanding "why" I was chosen to hear and understand God's words. I was still in the, "I am going to die mode," and, honestly, now believed God came to me so I would not be afraid of the journey he had planned.

Considering I had no clients, I then decided to go for a walk in the park with my ten-year-old son, Jesse. God's voice again came to me. This time through Jesse's mouth. As we walked, God told me, "He had a plan for all of us." He said, "trust in him and, do not have fear. Children are precious gifts, and He will always take care of them here on Earth and in Heaven." I played with Jesse while he swung on a swing for a short time, then we found our way home. I never again received a message through my son.

Jesse's dad came to pick him up a short time after and I began to feel an overwhelming weakness and decided to lay on my bed for a while. Marco arrived to check on me thinking my behavior mercurial. Unbeknownst to me, my telephone was not working. Therefore, no one was able to contact me. Apparently, there was never a message from my co-workers stating, I had no clients that day. When I hadn't shown up for work or answered the phone, two of my good friends, Jan and Jordan, appeared at the door to see if I was in trouble and found me lying in bed. Marco was still there, and he told the girls I had been acting strangely. I informed them I did not want to get out of bed and was just waiting there for God to come and take me. I was adamant, and just knew, I was dying!

At the same time, this phenomenon was happening to me, Ceaira was at her home in Virginia. She was the one dying, but I had no idea regarding the forthcoming tragedy. She had been bedridden for a week and had become more ill by the hour. Her boyfriend, Connor, had tried to persuade her to visit the doctor, but she refused to listen to his pleas.

Back at my house, I continued to refuse to get out of bed, emphasizing to all how great God was; and, subsequently decided to share the last few days secret discussions with God, Jesus to my friends. At this point, the two asked me if I was on drugs. Again, I was adamant; I was not! The only explanation they had for me 'I had gone crazy'. Everyone began to search the cabinets looking for a cache. The trash was no exception in their search. Nothing was found. Feeling vindicated, I returned to the prone position as, once again, weakness overcame my now fragile body and mind.

The rummaging through my home and personal items, by people who were my friends, sparked the dormant energy in my body to rise to full and elevated anxiety. I was not crazy or delusional. My anger at their belief I was taking drugs, and the intrusion of personal items, was now more significant than their suspicion.

Angered, I overcame the desire to lay there to wait for death. Lethargically, but with the fury of inner mental strength, I again pulled myself out of bed to show there was nothing in my house remotely related to legal or illegal drugs. Unless of course, Tylenol put me in this state. I proceeded to help them in their search to locate any stimulants they thought I hid to prove my honor. I was not a liar. If I had ever lied, it could have been due to protect someone I loved or cared about. I may have even in the past unintentionally created a falsehood in the form of omission. But this was really big. My friends who were there for me trying to figure out what was happening to me would not catch me in a lie. I had integrity, and I was going to prove it.

My lover, Marco, and my friends had seen enough. Their actions had me shouting angrily. They all now believed I definitely went over the edge and, unapologetically, called 911. When the paramedics arrived, I refused to go to the Emergency Room. But, then, these best friends called the police, who were vigilant. Their mindset, 'surely this lady was nuts'. I was forced to go along in the ambulance and kicked and screamed like an animal in a trap. There were restraints on my arms and legs. Yes, I went along for the ride, but I was madder than I had ever been. And guess who was in the ambulance with me? Yes! God, Jesus. I looked up and there "He" was. "His" image in the lights on the ceiling of the vehicle. My best friend God, Jesus was now there to console me in a time of severe distress. God told me, "Do not to worry. He was here with me, in the lights." I heard Him in the sounds I was hearing and the air I breathed. He said, "I am with you and I am everything." God, then, told me, "Think of love and not be afraid." Mentally, I believed I was entirely in control, and God was by my side. "Hold on everybody".

Apparently, when I arrived at the hospital, the ER doctors thought it necessary to knock me out with a sleep drug. The next thing I knew, I was waking up in a hospital room, and my arms were strapped down. I learned from the nurse on duty I had put up such a fight, the staff thought I would hurt myself or try to leave. Of course, I don't remember being combative. While in the room, I could see clouds above me in the fluorescent lights. Again, God talked to me. "His" voice was clear. "He" was there.

Suddenly, I had the urge to urinate. What an ordinary act?! Here I was in God's light, and one of the most essential human functions became the priority while God was present. I then did become irate and began to yell for someone to come and take me to the bathroom. Not so lucky. I was brought a bedpan and forced to relieve myself while lying down in the light of God's presence. It felt so dehumanizing. I believe when I had to relieve myself, it was paralleling some of the same kidney dysfunction as Ceaira. Obviously two different experiences and outcomes. However, mother and child so close to each other's heart somewhat sharing a physical dilemma; Ceaira in crisis losing kidney function, all those hundreds of miles away.

Meanwhile in Virginia, again unbeknownst to me at the time, Ceaira's condition was deteriorating. I was later told her bodily functions had begun to shut down, and she had urinated in her bed and became unresponsive. Connor had called 911. When the ambulance arrived at the hospital, Ceaira was in a coma.

Now, we were both in the hospital at the same time. When the nurse came to take my blood, God, Jesus assured me the prick of the needle would not be the worst pain I would experience, and again told me, "'He' was with me and asked me to look at the clouds above my head." And, yes, there were clouds between the fluorescent lights clearly shaped as Angels wings. I noticed them floating upward. I had no idea at the time the arms may have represented my daughter on her way up to Heaven. Evidently, I had it all wrong. It was not me dying. Ceaira had left all of us. Could have our earthly connection been so intense and spiritually connected, I physically and mentally experienced all her sickness and her dying as though it was my own demise?

There was no clock where I lay supine in the hospital room. Time passed slowly and I had no idea how long I lay there. It seems I endured every type of test the doctors could think of to determine the drug they thought had allowed me the hysteria. They were going to find me out before I exited what I, at the time, believed to be imprisonment. Of course, all the tests were negative. No drugs were found in my system. I already knew it to be a fact. The hospital could no longer keep me. Huh! The doctors rationalized I merely had a massive panic attack. If they only knew? Evidently, if I had shared the phenomenal experience with the staff, I would have been transferred to a more secure institution. It was time to be quiet. And, I was.

Truthfully, those who are not opened to other worldly phenomenon, have no inclination to listen to those who have abstract ideas, thoughts or have experienced spiritual events: and especially those who have claimed visits from God. To this lot we are unusual, mentally deficit individuals. Science wants facts! If one does not see it, feel it or touch it, well, it is not real. But, every ounce of each experience in the last two weeks was mine. No, one can change my extraordinary visions. No one can tell me God wasn't there. He gave me too much information to be a non-believer. It is not unlike the person who claims they were abducted by aliens. Apparently, there appears to be a great deal of proof, or information regarding these other world creatures. Numerous video recordings of extraterrestrial crafts abound; but until one lands in a non-believing scientist backyard and he can see it with his own eyes, call in his/her cronies, document and take all the measurements, it will not be accepted. And, don't forget the aliens. They had better be in the craft; or, we will then be criticized for not admitting or acknowledging we were actually invaded by an adversarial planet, or whatever. My answer to anyone who questions my mental state, or is critical of my encounters, "I saw, what I saw." Amen!

Marco came to visit me before my release and was acting terribly anxious. He said, "We need to go to Virginia right away." Then he told me the worst news I would ever accept. Ceaira was definitely in the hospital and in a coma.

The doctors could find nothing physically wrong with me. I was immediately discharged. Marco rushed me home to pack a bag then stopped at my friend Cassie's. She was my closest friend at this time and could be counted on in a moment's notice. Cassie and I became immediate companions after the divorce with Matt. We were both in the same position and consistently leaned on each other for support. God was right when he said, "Angels would always be around me;" and Cassie definitely had her wings during this crisis. Both of these dear friends dropped everything: family, work, and all their other responsibilities to take me to my severely ill daughter.

"God is light, and in him, there is no darkness."

-John 1:5

King James Bible

Chapter Twenty-Nine
Fatal Destination

IT WOULD BE AN ELEVEN-HOUR drive through the black of night to reach our destination. I was so groggy and loopy from whatever medication the doctors had given me before leaving the hospital in Connecticut and slept through most of the trip. Perhaps, I was in some type of dream state. This may have also been part of God's plan. 'Keep her calm and quiet'. Throughout the drive, Marco stopped several times so all of us could stretch our legs and use the rest area restrooms. I remember we were going through one of the toll stations and searching through my purse for money to help pay. At the next area rest stop, I took my handbag with me so I could freshen up. I still felt groggy. It was the last time I remember seeing my wallet. I did not remember leaving it in the restroom until we arrived in Virginia.

During the drive, Cassie was trying to get me to eat something. I could not remember when I last had nourishment. I was not hungry. About halfway through the trip, Marco needed to stop, get some air and use a restroom. It was the middle of the night and he was exhausted. When he exited the car and got out, I awakened and said, "I'm dying. I'm dying, Cassie, I am dying." Cassie, yelled at me, "Amy, shut the hell up! You are not dying!" My actions in the last few weeks surely had taken a toll on all my dear friends. Between preaching about God and telling everyone I was dying. I must have surely left them thinking I was undoubtedly "one card short of a full deck."

Reluctantly, and with the disapproval of my declaration, Marco resumed his position at the wheel, and he drove on. Again, I fell asleep. However, I was later told it was only a short time when my cell phone rang. Marco and Cassie had been answering all the calls. This time when he answered he realized it was the physician at the hospital where Ceaira was being treated. Due to his accent, he handed the phone to Cassie. Like my mother's dreadful call many, many, years ago regarding my dad's passing; this time history repeated itself. It was the worst call I would never want to hear. But my friends were kind. They held off with the tragic news and later revealed the physician's words. The doctor had stated, to Cassie, "I'm sorry. We did everything we could, but she did not make it."

After the call, and after I had awakened everyone in the car was strangely silent during the last miles of the trip to Virginia. I know both my friends were sad. They had been determined to get me to Ceaira. Apparently, the events were meant to happen as they had. It does not make it any easier; they did not wake me during the journey to tell me she had passed away while I was sleeping. But I somehow already knew and kept it to myself during the heavy silence. I believed in the past several weeks, God's visits had prepared me for this day.

Chapter Thirty
Facing Tragedy in Virginia

IN THE EARLY MORNING OF the next day after my precious girl, Ceaira, passed away, we arrived at the hotel where we stayed. The three of us checked in to the room we shared, Marco and Cassie sat me down to tell me the sad news. They said, "Amy, she didn't make it. She passed away during the night." I looked at them and said, "I already knew. I felt her leave." Ceaira and I were always one. Of course, I knew. How could I not? I cried inconsolable, hysterically, primal cries coming from the bottom pit of your stomach, from your soul and from a mother who has lost a child. I was sick I wanted to vomit; then realized all the visions and conversations I had with God, Jesus were real. All the feelings I had of dying were not for me. It was not my fate. God was coming to take my daughter. I also believe the visions were a spiritual preparation. And the phenomena I was privy to had given me excellent guidance to educate me in the ways of the *Highest Power*. However, we do not always heed or accept what we learn.

After I learned from my dearest friends Ceaira was with God I began to have a feeling of peace permeate my being. The *Highest Power* was indeed my very best friend, and He was going to take care of Ceaira in Heaven. God takes care of all his children.

Not too long after, I realized my purse was missing. I had no money or credit cards. Thankfully, my friends took it upon themselves to finance me and said, "We will take care of whatever you need." I was not prepared for a funeral and would require a lot of money to pay for the expenses facing me in the next several days. Thankful for the kindness of my friends, I did not allow the missing purse to be a priority and gave into their generosity. Later, I would face the irony of losing my purse. It was a small problem compared to what I had to deal with during this tragedy. However, I am sure my friends again worried about my sanity. "Now she lost her purse," I could have almost heard the words.

Senseless through the next few days, my present surroundings were surreal. The entire time in Virginia, my mind was in a state of flux. Each physical movement I made was slow and unsure. I thought of myself as a mime. Although I knew God was with Ceaira and me; the human instinct in me took over. It was as though I was still asleep having a nightmare. I longed to really sleep, forever.

God had tried to prepare me. I was confident in this thought. But, at this time I needed him with me every minute of each hour. Where was "He" now?" I needed to hear "His" voice and see him. Yes, previous to my child's death he told me "He" was with me always. And I wanted and needed assurance. "Where are you, God?"

Eventually, Marco drove us to the hospital. When we arrived and talked with the doctor who had cared for my child, he explained Ceaira had been extremely ill due to a bacterial infection. Without her realizing, and thinking she had the flu each day the disease manifested itself as the weeks wore on. Refusing to visit the doctor or go to the emergency room, she was unaware during those days she was critically ill; and, ultimately, caused her own death. By the time she was admitted to the hospital, there was little hope for her recovery. Ceaira's heart surgery had only been a few months earlier, and my sweet girl was fragile. However, she was also stubborn and willful. By waiting too long to seek care, Ceaira had now crossed over to another dimension where I could no longer physically reach her.

Apparently, the implanted defibrillator had been annoying her, and while in Virginia Ceaira had had it removed by another physician. I did not agree with her decision. Before she had decided to do this, I asked her to come home to Connecticut to have the doctor she knew do the surgery. However, she was now with her dad's physician and believed she was in good hands. When I asked the doctor if the infection came from the surgery, he said there was no way to know. It could have come from a dirty spoon. I was asked if I wanted an autopsy, I said, "No." It would not bring her back, so there was no need. People who were aware of her history thought I should sue the operating doctor. In my heart, I knew everything happening was meant to be.

The next time we returned to the hospital and began to make arrangements for the funeral, I could hardly speak. Thankfully, by this time, friends and family began to arrive to help me get through my desperation. I was unprepared to take on the present responsibilities at hand. Throughout this catastrophic time, I believe being human had been one of the toughest challenges given to us by The Creator. Living was pure torture. Humans are filled with enormous love and emotion, but when logic is challenged during great suffering thinking rationally is never guaranteed.

It was ludicrous to allow myself to think through the notion I would need an outfit presentable for a wake. Just the thought of Ceaira laying in suspended animation was in itself excruciating. What an insurmountable task; mourning my child. The entire process was one big blur. How could a mother even deal with such a tragedy? There was no choice. Raw emotions were scalded by this most catastrophic reality.

My mom, who only lived down the street from Ceaira, was grieving so much I worried about her physical health. She had a slew of illnesses and disabilities. Ceaira had planned to move in with her Grandmother in a few weeks. Mom felt guilty. She had not physically visited Ceaira to see how she was coming along due to her own infirmities.

While I lived in this new surreal plane through the tragedy, everyone close to me did an excellent job helping to get the wake and funeral together in such a short period of time. One of my best friends from childhood, who was also Ceaira's godmother, Carene and her mom, drove to Virginia from Atlanta and had organized an enormous collage of pictures to honor Ceaira. It was displayed on a table in the reception area of the funeral home. I would have preferred looking at the photos while she was alive rather than her lifeless body in a casket open to all.

It was the most horrific view I had ever endured in my life. To me, she did not even resemble my precious daughter. Ceaira's face was swollen, and the makeup resembled a clown. When I looked down at her I could not have seen a worse sight. Anxiety, depression, and a feeling of unreality overpowered my senses; and these emotions were rising by the seconds.

"Was I in a nightmare?" I asked myself the question so many times during this horrible tragedy. "Please God," I asked, "Take her out of here. This is all wrong." My insides were continuously roiling, and I dry heaved this unbearable actuality. My heart and soul were blown to bits. Those around me, did not see my exploding and destructing brain. I was alone in my torment. My son, Jesse, was young; and perhaps he had a better chance to adjust to the loneliness and loss of Ceaira. I accepted my life had changed forever. Although I had fair warning, I was terribly hurt by my "best friend God, Jesus's" unpardonable act to take my child with him. I knew he took Ceaira because she was suffering in this life. If her heart condition did not take her life; perhaps her addiction to opioids may have.

During the nightmare, I decided I would never remember Ceaira as she looked in the casket. I detached the vision as if it never existed. The person in the box was simply not her. I genuinely believe her spirit had left her body when she actually passed away. And, now, she was with God, whom I remember, promised, "He takes care of all 'His' children on Earth and in Heaven." I choose to remember my precious daughter when she was alive and full of energy; when her smile landed on my eyes while we danced together around the house giving me the best part of my day. I will always remember Ceaira when her heart and body were not broken. I will always remember the sound of her voice. I will always remember all of her beauty and her warmth. I WILL ALWAYS REMEMBER!

Her funeral was dreadfully sad. So many people loved her. Her personality came through even in death. No one forgot how silly she was; her incredible lust for life and her theatrics when she accosted people to watch her sing and dance. In life, my child continuously sought places where there was joyful commotion. In respect, she was, undoubtedly, more like me. Many friends had traveled from Connecticut to say goodbye. I could see the pain in their faces, knowing they would never physically see their best friend again. Their sadness made me all the sadder and more distressed. The crying in the room was an unwavering whimper.

Her brother, Jesse was only ten years old at the time. He was probably the saddest of them all. My mom and one of my brothers, Larry, the most sentimental, were not doing well. Both had been drinking a great deal of alcohol to get through the tragedy. I was so worried about them and subconsciously angry they chose this time to indulge.

Cassie was astonished at how I was trying to take care of everyone else when others should have been taking care of me. I suppose I was not in my right mind, disoriented, overwhelmed, and tortured by my loss. Taking care of others is not what I remember; however, caring for my family was a normal instinctive trait for me. I always wanted everyone happy and safe. I suspect, unknowingly, I was on a mission to relieve all of the pain before my eyes and distract me from the current reality.

The evening after the funeral, we returned to the hotel. I could sense Ceaira's presence everywhere. She seemed to be a veil on my skin and a subtle force within me. When I turned on the TV for relief from my depressed mind, her favorite movie, *Marley and Me,* stared me in the face. I thought I was hallucinating. I then decided it was time to take a shower and switched off the droning sound. It had become an intrusive electric magnet bringing me into a place so full of sorrow I was in physical pain. Shortly after, while blow-drying my hair, sparks from this electrical device flew everywhere! It was ludicrous! Ceaira regularly stole my hair dryer to use for herself. I knew she was stalking me from the dimension where her soul now resided; and, to my disbelief, suddenly the device brought me a sense of peace and made me chuckle.

I decided to have Ceaira buried in Virginia. She was born there, and she would be by her father in rest in the cemetery facing the front door where Harley and I married. Instinctively, I knew she wanted to be close to him. Some people thought I should take her back to Connecticut to have her buried. But unlike me, Ceaira seemed to always be tethered to her roots. I believe, I know exactly what she would have wanted. And, as usual, I gave Ceaira anything I could to make her happy.

Do Not Stand at My Grave and Weep

Do not stand at my grave and weep
I am not there; I do not sleep.
I am in a thousand winds that blow,
I am the softly falling snow.
I am the gentle showers of rain,
I am the fields of ripening grain.
I am in the morning hush,
I am in the graceful rush
Of beautiful birds in circling flight
I am the starshine of the night.
I am in the flowers that bloom,
I am in a quiet room.
I am in the birds that sing,
I am in each lovely thing.
Do not stand at my grave and cry,
I am not there. I did not die

-Attributed to May Elizabeth Frye, 1932
This poem is in the public domain.
YourDailyPoem.com

Prior to Ceaira passing on February 4th, 2011,
this was her last Facebook post.

"it feels good just to tell God thanks for everything I have, try it ; -)"

Chapter Thirty-One
A Small Miracle

THE MORNING AFTER THE FUNERAL, Marco, Cassie and I packed our bags and begun our journey back to where I lived in Connecticut. None of us had much to say on the trip home. We were all horrifically grieved. I knew each of us was trying to reconcile with the devastating events of the last few days. I am so grateful for the friendship and support of Marco, and Cassie; as well as Carene, who needed to return to college in Atlanta. Everyone including Carene's mother had to get back to her life. Without their help, I would not only have been lost, but also, unable to navigate through the tragedy. God had retreated. I consoled myself with the belief I was sure he was helping someone with a pretty similar intolerable tragedy. I am also sure he directed the fateful plan. He said he would not leave me. I believe he was there through the love of my dear and most supportive friends.

I chastised myself for leaving my purse in, possibly, the restroom of the rest area on our way to Virginia. We tried to remember the place where we had stopped on the journey, constantly looking out the windows trying to pinpoint our stop just days before, however, they all look similar. It was ludicrous to think we could remember. However, anyway the three of us were stymied and grief-stricken by the events. For just a moment this task allowed for distraction, however, my purse was gone and so was Ceaira. We reconciled to the fact our search was an act of futility. The night was dark, and we were on the opposite side of the highway.

Actually, we were unable to reason. Grief tends to leave us in a mindless, brainless void. The voyage continued, and I told my friends I would deal with it when I reached home.

Close to home, I began to realize I needed to call all the creditors and cancel cards. Under such horrific events it is entirely ironic to be compelled to take a 360 degree turn of the brain to try and locate my purse and take control of normal everyday issues. The entire tragedy had been insufferable, however, although, I knew I had to live; I just wanted to die. How? I kept telling myself. 'one does not have the opportunity to just give up on ordinary tasks, no matter the tragedy'.

When we finally arrived in Connecticut, Marco first dropped off Cassie. Then he and I ventured to my apartment. When we realized the front door was locked and had no keys, we circled the house searching for an unlocked window. Thankfully, we were able to get in through the bathroom window. Marco lifted me up and gently hurled me through. Luckily, I am small and just about fit.

Once in, I unlocked the front door, and Marco entered. I looked towards the kitchen table and there sat my purse. I was stymied. This could not be. When I eyed Marco, he followed, and his face showed disbelief. Frankly, he looked terribly frightened. I, on the other hand, was joyful, grateful and open to the mystery. Why shouldn't I be? I had seen God. Therefore, nothing was impossible. It seemed like a miracle. Perhaps the angels flew it in. I believe it was just another undeniable phenomenon. However, it arrived I will never know.

I absolutely know my purse was in my hands when we left for Virginia. It is practically hot glued to my body. My cell was in my purse, and I remembered it ringing and passing it to Marco. He remembered answering my cell. My cousin had called me, but I was in no condition to talk to anyone while on the trip. I had also searched for change while going through toll booths, and my keys were there as we searched for more items.

This was another extraordinary event but also a blessing. I did not need to cancel credit cards. Immediately, I placed a call to Cassie to let her hear the news. Although shocked, she knew and had seen it with her own eyes as we journeyed to the fatal destination. How could have this strange incident happened? I don't know. We don't know. Or, perhaps I do. Actually, there is no reasonable explanation. Skeptics may reject these unusual events. My belief is it is a little miracle from God to remind me "He" has always had my back and still will be there.

Chapter Thirty-Two
Reflecting

For a short time after Ceaira's death, I randomly escaped into a surreal world I had conjured up for myself. In reality, if it was just a nightmare and she was gone, I would soon wake up, and life would be the same as before. Perhaps a world of imagination one lives in can prevent insanity. Sometimes denial can become one's best friend. Just the thought about Ceaira being left underground made me want to wretch. I would never see her beautiful face or hear her laughing voice again. Yes, I had invented the fantasy to soothe my tortured soul. However, I also sincerely believe God will protect my precious girl, but I just missed her too much.

Ironically, the only rationale I could understand through this desperation of loss was my private time with God before her death. The words he shared with me seemed to echo, "His" vibrant voice in my tangled brain. I needed God, Jesus presence severely. Somehow, I knew He wasn't coming back. I just knew. It was a feeling.

The pain of the loss of my daughter was indescribable. My heart was bleeding, my soul was crushed, and I cry tears for eternity. My baby girl was the very first person who had given me the gift of pure love and was no longer a human figure in my life. Except for my prior visits from God, I was lost. The time has passed, and I now realize why when a loved one has left the Earth, God leaves us with memories. I believe I have been left with a beautiful remembrance of a child who was my first greatest love.

After having time spent with God before Ceaira passed, I now know he was there all along. He had placed people in my life like Carene, Aunt Louise, Cousin Susan, Cassie, Marco and all the other members of my dad's family, as well as other close friends to keep me safe. And my dad, who had visited me in spirit so long ago.

Although I could not physically see God his voice was loud and clear. Yes! "He" was there. I also truly believe he was my imaginary best friend when I was a child and "He" continued "His" friendship with me through friends and relatives. I know I will be "His" best friend in the future and, hopefully, "He" will continue to care and protect me. The difference now is I see God in all living things. I also believe there is a piece of God in all living things. We are all connected to God, and it is up to us to open our eyes to see him, listen to him, and open our hearts to "His" magnificence. It may be difficult; however, I believe in conversing with God in our human world is extraordinary.

Ceaira's spirit is always with me. My heart knows this fact. The image of her sweet face is forever a photograph on my brain, and her soul resonates with mine. I do not feel the need to go to a place in the ground to visit. She is here. I feel her soul.

Chapter Thirty-Three
The Odds Were Against Us

AFTER I LOST MY GIRL, it took a long while for me to help myself navigate away from a surreal world. It is difficult to find a level of comfort when one deals with grief. Grief is uncomfortable. Emotions were so high; I merely went along with decisions others made for me. When a soul is fragile, it tends to seek comfort from wherever it is given. I decided to give-in to Marco's demands to make a commitment to our relationship. After all, if I could live through losing my precious child, nothing should stand in my way. I could reach for the love, and lover I wanted and yearned for without recriminations from family and friends. It was my life, and of course, his. We could have made our stand and devoted our love to each other. However, again, I am sure Marco's family ties were stronger than his love for me. His family always gave him a terrible time about our relationship.

Although Marco was adamant regarding the need to be with me forever, he was so stressed out between the need, and loyalty he had for his ethnic family, the guy was drowning in his own sorrow. I realized after all Marco had done for me, I wanted to be with him forever. I said to him, "I want to keep you now." He replied, "let's just live in the moment and see what happens." The decision was made to commit to the relationship permanently; however, he was hammocking under terrible pressure to split his time between the blood relatives and me. The guilt he felt was enormous. And, honestly, I shared his sorrow.

Finally, again, logic took over. We both faced the inevitable. After being together for three years, we ended our relationship. Not only did I lose my daughter, but my lover and best friend. Many times, in the past I tried every maneuver I could to disconnect from him. Now, knowing he had made a choice with me to end our love affair, I believed another piece of my soul had been eaten away. Our relationship may have been connected by time and tragedy, but we could not escape reality. And, the truth is hard to deny. The decision to end our affair had forever been settled by logic.

Marco and I had been together for two years when Ceaira passed away. And another year before our love affair finally took its toll on his family, him, and me. They were just not going to welcome me with open arms, and I was not going to walk down the aisle with my incredible lover. Nor would I receive the bouquet of palms from his mother, a custom of his heritage when a woman is accepted into a matriarch's family. It was all over. His family had won. However, perhaps so had I. Although I had never liked all the odds, we had against us, they were actually the reasons our life together in permanence could never be. This tender-hearted man was the steel through each catastrophe I endured with Ceaira, up to and including, her death. He was also there before Ceaira's passing when I believed I was the one dying.

Chapter Thirty-Four
Jesse, My Forever Best Man

MY SON, JESSE, IS A special boy. I am so grateful he belongs to me. I thank Matt for giving him to me. Jesse had also been the stalwart man who helped me to keep moving forward and living life when I didn't think I was able. My boy was ten years old when his sister, Ceaira, passed away. It was naturally hard for him to understand his emotions through the loss of her. But he is strong, and the support he received from his dad made his grief a little more manageable. Sometimes Jesse makes such mature comments regarding life. I look at him and think *what an old soul.*

It wasn't too long after Ceaira's passing, Jesse and I went to see the movie, *Pirates of the Caribbean.* Ceaira and I loved watching the actor Johnny Depp in all his films. We both had a crush on him. When the movie was over, I started to cry while thinking about how she would have loved to have seen this movie with her brother and me. I tried not to let Jesse see my tears because I did not want him to think I loved him less then I loved Ceaira. Overwrought, I was unable to hold back. I explained to him why I was sobbing, and his response was, "Mom, we just have to act like she is still in Virginia and know in our hearts she is always with us." He made me smile. My young boy found his own way of dealing with the loss of her, and I believe he shared this idea with me to give me courage. God gave me an incredible son. Although tragedy affected me ruthlessly, I had been blessed with this young man of mine.

Poem for Jesse

What a Boy
What a Joy
The Lord of my Manor
That's who you are
A Bright Light in your mother's eyes
Although a boy always very wise
You have always been a Shining Knight
I know this when I kiss you goodnight
I am so happy to have you here
And, I will do my best to keep you near
You are such a handsome dear
Be safe, be healthy, Be Happy, Be True
God gave you such wisdom
This I knew

~Michele L Shriver, Author

Someone once said,
"When the student is ready. The teacher will arrive."
"When the Seeker is ready, the Master will appear."

~ *(Buddhist Proverb) (Theosophical)*

Chapter Thirty-Five
Reality

As time moved forward, and I began feeling alone and lonely it was not unusual for me to again indulge a couple of glasses of wine before going to bed. The tragedy had triggered insomnia. On occasion, when I accompanied new friends from work to an event, I would begin talking about Ceaira and all the good memories. But when I arrived home, I just cried hysterically until the emotional exhaustion willed me to sleep. Although I loved God, and believed in him infinitely, I am also a human being with all the flaws and negative characteristics. I was in complete utter pain and agony. I wanted my girl with me. I wanted to hug, hold and smell her. My pain was excruciating torture. To live without her would be torture. I bargained with God, and asked, 'Why'?

It took a great deal of time and strength, however, navigating as best I could through daily life, ultimately managing with great difficulty, to change my lifestyle after losing my precious Ceaira. Finding a way to the day to day realities of life became a mission to save myself from all the human insecurities facing me. The regular bar scene had come to a halt. It wasn't fun anymore. Most of the things I thought were important in my life became ludicrous to me. I could see who my real friends were. The people who accompanied me on my nighttime forays of having fun never called or visited anymore. I determined they were not interested in me as a friend, but as a good-time girl. We no longer had any interests in common.

At a point of committal to myself, I did not want to drink anymore.

Again, I began to remember the wonderful time spent with God. His words to me resonated over and over about not hiding my pain, and not to be afraid to love. There was no reason to fear love. I believe "He" knew how I felt about my young lover and had decided he would allow me to deal with these emotions in my own time. During our first meeting, God said, "He would always be with me through life's hard times, and with 'Him', I need nothing else." After truly focusing on this memory of God's declaration, this message finally and definitely sunk into my brain, I completely quit using alcohol. I do not miss it. I especially do not miss the hangover. Losing Ceaira is far worse than any other pain I had and would ever experience.

Her love throughout the years had kept me strong most of my life. I was bent on making sure she traveled the right road. Her addiction gave me pain. Ceaira's death nearly annihilated my soul with an unrepairable hole in my heart. I could have gone a different, and destructive route after Ceira's death. She would have been so disappointed in me if I used her death to take the wrong path in life. So, I choose to have God, as my best friend, to get me through all the pain and sadness. What more do I need?

A long-time after the loss of Ceaira I met an old friend of my daughter's. She stated, "I first moved here to Connecticut where I entered seventh grade. I knew no one. Your daughter came up to me at the bus stop and introduced herself. She had the biggest smile on her pretty face and asked me to sit with her on the bus. Then, she introduced me to some of her friends and asked me to sit with her at lunchtime. She made my first day so much easier. I will never forget her." And that was my Ceaira, friendly, loving and kind.

After the breakup with Marco, we attempted to remain just friends, but it was too hard. There was irresistible chemistry between us. At random times after our huge breakup when Marco and I ran into each other after the split, we momentarily relapsed into the same old sexual encounters. I was not looking for a "friends with benefits" relationship so, again, we eventually distanced ourselves from one another.

Marco and I both believed our decision to end our relationship was agonizing. My entire body reacted to the finality of our choice. As time progressed, he would call and ask me irrelevant questions, "Could I get him some special hair product? Could I fit him in for a haircut?" His desire to see me became difficult and bizarre for us both. Occasionally, the emotional feelings would resurrect themselves. However, I had to act diligently to solidify my commitment. To STOP the reeling fantasy in my brain became distressing while I longed for him. Of course, I felt sick after every phone call. And the feeling became stronger each time. To me it is like drinking alcohol or any other addiction.

Occasionally, I would see and talk to his sister, Lanie. She was a client of mine at the beauty salon where I worked. When she mentioned him, it was internal misery. I decided to block their cell phone numbers so the pain would go away. In the past when my Ceaira was in the hospital having her surgery for the insertion of the pacemaker Lanie and Marco's mother were very good to us. They brought food to the hospital as well as inviting me to dinner at their home. But it was the extent of their love and kindness for me.

Although I consider Lanie a friend and I know she cares for me, she also wants her brother to marry someone his own age and ethnicity. I am not angry with her choice. She is probably wiser than me. I cannot have him!

Then one day, after many months I ran into Marco. I am sure it was deliberate on his part. We talked and decided to go to dinner and catch up. Instantly, it was as though we had never left each other. I admitted blocking his number, and how it had helped me deal with the detachment. And, determined to widen the gap told him my feelings for him had diminished. It was a lie. I knew I loved him even more. We ended our dinner and went our separate ways. I had to get him completely out of my life if I was going to survive. It has now been many years since we ended our love affair. If I fall in love with anyone the way I did with Marco, age will not matter within reason of course. I believe love has no age. True love is rare and if I am lucky to find it again, I will not let it pass by me, young or old.

Although we are not together and my heart has been bruised, I will always be grateful for Marco's love and support through my worst times. He was the most tenderhearted man I ever knew, the steel through all the devastation I experienced with Ceaira. Perhaps there was a way to work on a plan to keep our friendship alive, but I had fooled myself for so long; it was time to grow up. My belief is, God sometimes places people in our lives for a reason unknown to us, even if they will not be with us forever.

"And When I loved You,
I Realized I Never Truly Loved Anyone
I Realized I Never Will Truly Love Anyone
The Way I Love You"

Author Unknown

Chapter Thirty-Six
Afterthoughts

W HEN CEAIRA PASSED, MY BLOOD family did not or could not help me financially. Marco had paid for much of Ceaira's funeral cost. I don't believe he helped because he had to, but because he cared for me. He is a good man with a good heart. Assuming there was some hope to have a life together had perhaps been a fantasy of my making. I have not dated anyone in many years. Yes, I am open to a good, stable relationship. However, I have not seen or spoken to any man who roused my passion or curiosity. I know now what real love is. If I never find the kind of love I had with Marco, I am okay with it. My belief is I am genuinely lucky to have known a special man's love even for a brief time in my life. Staying busy with good reliable friends, and frequently traveling to other countries with these special people has become my new passion; and finding enormous joy in raising my son, Jesse, affords me the greatest pleasure and comfort. Perhaps Jesse is and always will be the man in my life. Sometimes, I still think about the playmate no one, but I could see when I was a child. I now believe it was most likely God, Jesus. After all, He did say, "I will be with you always."

The pure love emanating from His presence was and is unexplainable. For me, being with God was a glimpse of the perfection one must see when entering Heaven. There had been no fear with the visits from God, Jesus just a permeable sensation of unconditional love. From Him

I received the extraordinary knowledge Ceaira did not suffer through the ravaging illness but transitioned into God's loving care for all eternity.

Yes, it has taken me a long time to successfully navigate through my fractured life, at times a terrifying and somewhat regretful life. Then, there were times of great joy. As I mentioned early on living in The *House of Madness* with abuse and fear on a daily basis, causes one to make some dire, and spontaneous undesirable choices and decisions. Although many will scrutinize the experience of my life events with the connection to the *Higher Power* I say, "we are all connected in some way to God, Jesus." *He* lives within all of us. It is a matter of our acceptance of his "love and our faith" two of the most powerful components in our relationship with him.

I often ask myself why I was chosen. Why did "He" come to me in the ways "He" did? This remains unanswered for me. Again, it is beyond my comprehension. Perhaps a theological scholar has a reasonable answer. I surely do not. Although I may be entirely off track, my personal explanation is, "from the beginning, I always needed God in my life to help me through the dysfunction and horrific events, as well as my unreasonable choices', God was always there." His unorthodox presence in my life, unfortunately, culminated with the most horrific tragedy I would witness. Each time "He" arrived; I accepted his loving presence. When Ceaira died, I again became surreal to the physicality of the real world and needed the vision of 'Him to return. In life we do not always get what we want when we want, however, if we can get some peace within our souls there will always be hope for the future.

I know terrible events happen to people every day and God does not show up to help them. The fact is, without immediate help from a *Higher Power*, people sometimes reject his likelihood. Many individuals struggle through life. Most often those who mentally survive devastating experiences they suffer seem to always find a way to help others. Perhaps these individuals already have "the connection." to *God*, and love, the mysteries of the Universe

Beloved, let us love one another for love is from God,
and whoever loves had been born of God and knows God.

John 4:7

Beloved are the eyes that see what others cannot see.

Luke 10:23

For My Precious Daughter Ceaira

Without her here it's been very, very cold
I miss her so much, "she will be loved" I've been told
You took her away from her mother's fold
If the plan is bigger than me, I'll trust you
You promised you would take care of her
I hope you do
A daughter so loved I cannot replace
But, now you have her in your embrace
I miss and cherish her lovely face
You said you would take care
I remember when you said it, and I think of
your words each night before bed
So, again please keep her safe, You said you would
I'd take her back in a second if I thought I could
Your world is hers now
That I understood
When you took her away, you didn't ask me if it was okay
She is probably flying around like a free honeybee
I think her spirit is free
When you took her, did you fix her heart?
It was not very good right from the start
This mother has accepted to give you the reign
Although you taking her gives me great pain
I'll revere you and pray to you every single day
To make sure she is happy and always feeling gay

~Michele Shriver, Author

Epilogue

NAVIGATING THROUGH LIFE, I PERSONALLY learned our decisions and choices determine every aspect of our worldly expedition. For my mom it began with the worst decision she ever made when she married Lenny, her second husband. I also personally managed some pretty reckless decisions and choices throughout my adulthood. Ceaira made a life-threatening decision when she chose to have her pacemaker removed. Unfortunately, for my family and me, we all made really terrible decisions and choices with heartbreaking results. Living with the consequences of premature ill-considered decisions and choices of our making are usually the cause of a person's lifelong dilemmas. *Free-will* can be a disagreeable gift we are given at birth. It can also be the most gratifying. Our options to satisfy favorable outcomes are endless. However, we all have the propensity to take destructive paths. Some of us believe the route looking easy to endeavor is the way to go. In truth, I later learned the easy path is the most difficult to travel. Whereas, thinking through the most difficult course can result in a more fulfilled life. At least, I *believe,* I finally learned this *truth* navigating through my personal fears and struggles.

Moreover, I realize at the time of our birth, we do not receive a contract guaranteeing us immortality. Through my life experiences, I also came to the personal conclusion and learned immortality is a surety only after we leave this plane and embark on our journey to *The Higher Place.* This belief I personally aspire to is surely the most challenging truth to accept, recognize and understand. The connection between man and God, and *The Universe* is personal. We are all only characters in this "fantasy life" with the people we know, care about and love. And all of us are just fragile souls, moving along, sometimes slowly, and at other times chaotically to the unknown; the actual destination, *The Higher Place,* the place where I have been told by a *Higher Power,* we are finally safe, forever.

It has been several years since my precious daughter, Ceaira, passed away. She died on February 28, 2011, at the age of twenty, one month before her twenty-first birthday. My life now, and the way I viewed the concept of living in the past, has changed significantly. The idealistic priorities I imagined for Ceaira to living a perfect life were shattered with the loss of my precious child. The ideal plans I had for a perfect family life, peace and security regarding myself and the future for Ceaira had somewhat failed me. In life I tried to reach for the moon, and for a moment landed on a falling star, Ceaira. Now, it is the presence of my son, Jesse, another star, who gives me comfort, strength, and the ability to again see a future of hope.

I always believed I had the power to control life's unfairness, and miseries by assuming a kind and loving spirit. Now, I realize no human has this power. Although, I had momentous encounters with The Higher Spirit after Ceaira left I as a human lost the desire to accept reality. I was most definitely not ready to accept her leaving this earth permanently. The truth is, *she did not belong to me.* And, too early her spirit had transcended to a parallel universe. The perfect life I envisioned with Ceaira, is now in a category of grains of sand, blown away by her physical disappearance. I can only love her spirit from afar.

I am indeed not unique; just another human being made to wade through the many hauntings, chaos, and tragedies of life.

Now I navigate the future without fear. Strength and faith are my strategies to survive.

And, by the Grace of God, I survived "them", my haywire family, and the tragic loss of my precious daughter, Ceaira.

Amy Lynn

To publicly share the terrible events Amy Lynn experienced in childhood and as an adult, as well as, her connection to proclaim her connection to "God" is simply her way to give help and hope for others.

It has been my honor to Author Amy Lynn's book and "to ultimately share her truth."

Gratitude to my daughter, Elisa Ann Liptak, whose heart understands, and for support, encouragement, and assistance while writing this story.

Author, Michele Accardi, Shriver

Made in the USA
Monee, IL
19 November 2020